HATCHMENTS IN BRITAIN

I

Northamptonshire, Warwickshire

and Worcestershire

1

Northamptonshire, Warwickshire and Worcestershire

Edited by

PETER SUMMERS, F.S.A.

PHILLIMORE

1974

Published by

PHILLIMORE & CO. LTD.

London and Chichester

Head Office: Shopwyke Hall

Chichester, Sussex, England

ISBN 0 85033 085 8

Text set in 9pt. Baskerville by Phillimore

Printed and bound in Great Britain at
The Camelot Press Ltd, Southampton

CONTENTS

ILLUSTRATIONS

GENERAL INTRODUCTION

Hatchments are a familiar sight to all those who visit our parish churches. They are not only decorative, but of great interest to the herald, genealogist and local historian. It is therefore surprising that — apart from local surveys in a few counties mostly in recent years — no attempt has yet been made to record them on a national scale. This series will, it is hoped, remedy the deficiency; it is proposed to publish separate volumes covering all English counties as well as Wales, Scotland and Ireland.

It is probable that no volume will be complete. Previously unrecorded hatchments will turn up from time to time; many have already been found in obscure places such as locked cupboards and ringing chambers. There are likely to be some inaccuracies, for hatchments are often hung high up in dark corners, and the colours may have faded or be darkened with age and grime. Identification is a problem if the arms do not appear anywhere in print: and even if the arms are identified, pedigrees of the family may not always be available. But enough has been done to make publication worth while; the margin to the pages will perhaps allow for pencilled amendments and notes.

Since I began the survey in 1952 many hatchments, probably evicted at the time of Victorian restorations, have been replaced in the churches whence they came. On the other hand, during the same period just as many hatchments have been destroyed. An excuse often made by incumbents is that they are too far gone to repair, or that the cost of restoration is too great. Neither reason is valid. If any incumbent, or anyone who has the responsibility for the care of hatchments which need attention, will write to me, I shall be happy to tell him how the hatchments may be simply and satisfactorily restored at a minimal cost. It is hoped that the publication of this survey will help to draw attention to the importance of these heraldic records.

The diamond-shaped hatchment, which originated in the Low Countries, is a debased form of the medieval achievement — the shield, helm, and other accoutrements carried at the funeral of a noble or knight. In this country it was customary for the hatchment to be hung outside the house during the period of mourning, and thereafter be placed in the church. This practice, begun in the early 17th century, is by no means entirely obsolete, for about 80 examples have so far been recorded for the present century.

Closely allied to the diamond hatchment, and contemporary with the earlier examples, are rectangular wooden panels bearing coats of arms. As some of these bear no inscriptions and a black/white or white/black background, and as some otherwise typical hatchments bear anything from initials and a date to a long inscription beginning 'Near here lies buried . . .', it will be appreciated that it is not always easy to draw a firm line between the true hatchment and the memorial panel. Any transitional types will therefore also be listed, but armorial boards which are clearly intended as simple memorials will receive only a brief note.

With hatchments the background is of unique significance, making it possible to tell at a glance whether it is for a bachelor or spinster, husband or wife, widower or widow. These different forms all appear on the plate immediately following this introduction.

Royal Arms can easily be mistaken for hatchments, especially in the West Country where they are frequently of diamond shape and with a black background. But such examples often bear a date, which proves that they were not intended as hatchments. Royal hatchments, however, do exist, and any examples known will be included.

All hatchments are in the parish church unless otherwise stated, but by no means are they all in churches; many are in secular buildings and these, if they have no links with the parish in which they are now found, are listed at the end of the text. All hatchments recorded since the survey began are listed, including those which are now missing.

For the substance of this volume, the first in the series, we are indebted to Mr. W.A. Peplow, Mr. R.J. Kitchin and the late Mr. G. A. Harrison, who have visited every church in their respective counties and recorded every hatchment. The illustrations are the work of Mr. Harrison and will provide an invaluable 'key' for those unfamiliar with the complexity of hatchment backgrounds.

Peter G. Summers
Day's Cottage, North Stoke, Oxford

1. MARRIED MAN

2. MARRIED WOMAN

3. BACHELOR

4. WIDOW

5. WIDOWER

6. SPINSTER

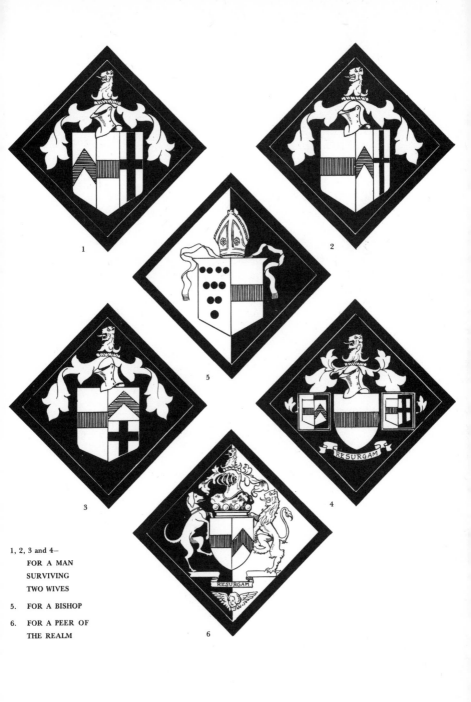

1, 2, 3 and 4—
   FOR A MAN
   SURVIVING
   TWO WIVES

5.   FOR A BISHOP

6.   FOR A PEER OF
     THE REALM

ABBREVIATIONS

B.P. = *Burke's Peerage, Baronetage and Knightage*
B.L.G. = *Burke's Landed Gentry*
B.E.B. = *Burke's Extinct and Dormant Baronetcies*
Grazebrook = H.S. Grazebrook, *History of Worcestershire*
   ( )
Baker = Baker, *History of Northamptonshire* (1822-41)
Markham = C.A. Markham, 'Hatchments', *Northampton and Oakham Architectural Society Proceedings*, Vol. XX, Pt. 2 (1912), 673-759.

NOTE

Blazons throughout are exactly as noted at the time of recording, not as they ought to be.

NORTHAMPTONSHIRE

Lois Weedon: For the Hon. Frederick Sylvester North Douglas, 1819

INTRODUCTION

In 1910, the Northamptonshire and Oakham Architectural Society published an article, The Hatchments of Northamptonshire, by Christopher Markham, F.S.A. This article contained full blazons and genealogical details of 134 examples.

In 1954, on hearing that a national survey of hatchments was being carried out, I decided to visit every church in the county, and carry out a careful check of Markham's findings. The results were most interesting; 13 of the hatchments recorded by Markham had disappeared, but I was able to record many more, most of which had previously been overlooked. I was able, at the same time, to correct a number of blazons which had been inaccurately noted. Altogether I added nearly 40 hatchments to Markham's list, but not all these were in churches. I have also photographed every hatchment, and these photographs have been invaluable in checking details.

Some of the earliest hatchments, dating from the first quarter of the 18th century, can be seen in the church at Canons Ashby. There are certainly two, possibly three, modern examples. At Deene there is a bachelor's hatchment, probably for James Ernest John Brudenell-Bruce, who died in 1917. The other two are for Sir Hereward Wake, Bt. at Courteenhall, who died in 1963, and for Sir Edward de Capell Brooke, Bt., at Great Oakley, who died in 1968. The last two were painted by Mr. C.B. Savage of Northampton, who has assisted me, not only in illuminating pedigrees (now hanging in the churches), which I drew up to illustrate the hatchments, but also in telling me of hatchments in private hands.

In the central library in Northampton there is a small silken hatchment to George Ives, 4th Baron Boston, who died in 1869. This was probably used at the funeral.

Finally, I must refer to two memorial panels, which closely resemble hatchments. The one at Stoke Bruerne to Jane

Nailour, d. 21st Jan. 1655/6, is remarkable in that the background is black only on the sinister side, correctly showing that she predeceased her husband. But it cannot be listed as a hatchment for it bears a lengthy inscription on a scroll below the arms, starting 'Here lyes interred . . .'; it was almost certainly made as a simple form of permanent memorial. The other, at Barnwell, is in memory of Elizabeth Smith, d. 3rd March, 1665.

R.J. Kitchin
Brook Cottage, Holcot, Northampton

ALDWINCLE

1. Sinister background black
Azure a cross of nine mascles argent between four eagles displayed or in sinister chief a small corbie proper (Spinckes), impaling, Vert on a chevron between three stags trippant or three trefoils slipped gules (Robinson)
Crest: A talbot passant gules bezanty gorged with four fusils argent
Mantling: Gules and argent
For Margaret, wife of Elmes Spinckes of Aldwincle.   She d. 16 June, 1717.   (Bridges, Northampton, ii., 211)

ASHBY ST. LEDGERS

1. Dexter background black
Azure a cinquefoil within a bordure engrailed ermine (Ashley), impaling, Chequy argent and gules a lion rampant guardant or (Pocock)
Crest: A harpy proper   Mantling: Gules and argent
Motto: Mors janua vitae
For John Bentley Ashley, who m. Jane Pocock, and d. 21 Sept. 1761.
(Baker, i. 246)

2. All black background
On a lozenge   Azure a cinquefoil argent within a bordure engrailed ermine (Ashley), impaling, Chequy argent and gules a lion rampant or (Pocock)
Motto: In coelo quies
For Jane, widow of John Bentley Ashley.   She d. 13 June 1784.

3. Dexter background black
Azure a cinquefoil inverted within a bordure engrailed ermine (Ashley), impaling, Sable three roses argent (Smith)
Crest: A harpy proper   Mantling: Gules and argent
For Joseph Ashley, who m. Jane, dau. of Capt. John Smith, of Workington, Cumberland, and d. 15 July 1798.   (Baker, i. 246)

4. All black background
On a lozenge   Ashley, as 1., impaling Smith, as 3.
For Jane, widow of Joseph Ashley.   She d. 13 Sept. 1828.
(Markham)

5. All black background
On a lozenge surmounted by a cherub's head
Qly of six, 1st, Or a popinjay proper in chief an annulet sable (Senhouse),

2nd, Gules three lucies hauriant two and one argent (Lucy), 3rd, Gules
a chevron between three combs argent (Ponsonby), 4th, Gules three
eagles displayed or (Eglesfield), 5th, Azure on a chevron or four roses
gules and in base a dolphin naiant embowed argent (   ), 6th, Gules a
fret argent (Fleming)   In pretence: Ashley, as 2.
For Mary, dau. and co-heir of Joseph Ashley, who m. 1787, Sir Joseph
Senhouse, and d. 2 Oct. 1850.   (B.L.G. 7th ed.)

6. Dexter background black
Gules a chevron ermine between three pheons or (Arnold)
Crest: A demi-tiger reguardant sable bezanty, holding between its paws
a pheon or
Mantling: Gules and ermine   Motto: Ut vivas vigila
Probably for George Arnold, who m. Anne, dau. and co-heir of Thomas
Bromwich of Daventry (probably non-armigerous) and d. 20 Feb.
1766.   (Baker i. 247)

7. All black background
Arnold, as 6.   In pretence: Argent five mascles fesswise in chief
gules and five fusils fesswise in base sable, all within a bordure argent
charged with roundels gules (Burgess)
Crest: As 6.   Mantling: Gules and ermine   Motto: Vivas ut vigila
For Lumley Arnold, the only son of George Arnold. He m. Anne, dau.
of James Burgess and d. 5 May 1781.   (B.L.G. 7th ed.)

8. Dexter background black
Qly, 1st and 4th, Arnold, 2nd and 3rd, Burgess   In pretence: Azure a
cinquefoil argent (? White)   Also impaling, Or on a cross sable five
fleurs-de-lys argent (Morrison)
Crest: As 6.   Mantling: Gules and ermine   Motto: Ut vivas vigila
For George Arnold, son of Lumley Arnold. He m. 1st, Elizabeth, dau.
and heiress of William White, of Wolvey, co. Warwick, who d. 10 March
1788. He m. 2nd, Jane, dau. of Lieut.-Gen. Morrison, of London,
and d. 24 Oct. 1806.   (Baker, i. 247)

BENEFIELD

1. Sinister background black
Shield surmounted by two cherubs' heads
Qly, 1st and 4th, Ermine a lion rampant gules plain collared or, on a
chief azure three roses argent barbed vert (Russell), 2nd and 3rd, Azure
a bend engrailed or ermined sable between two crescents or a canton
gules (Watts)   In pretence: (on dexter) Azure a bend engrailed or
ermined sable between two crescents or (Watts), and (on sinister), Argent
three bears' heads erased gules muzzled or (Barker)
For Maria Ellen, dau. of Peter Henry Barker, of Bedford, 2nd wife of

Jesse Watts-Russell, of Biggin House, Northants. She d. 30 Oct. 1844. (B.L.G. 2nd ed.)

BLATHERWICK

1. All black background
Qly, 1st and 4th, Per pale gules and or three lions passant guardant counterchanged (O'Brien), 2nd, Argent three piles gules (Bryan), 3rd, Argent a pheon azure (Sidney), over all a label of three points argent for cadency
Crest: Issuant from clouds a dexter arm embowed the hand grasping a sword in bend sinister proper
Mantling: Gules and or   Motto: Vigueur de dessus
Possibly for Augustus Stafford O'Brien Stafford, d.s.p. 1857.
(B.L.G. 7th ed.)

2. All black background (should be dexter black)
Qly, as 1., impaling, Or fretty gules a canton ermine (Noel)
Crest, mantling and motto: As 1.
For Stafford O'Brien, who m. 1808, Emma, dau. of Sir Gerard Noel, Bt. and d. 3 Mar. 1864. She d. 1873. (B.P. 1896 ed)

3. Dexter background black
Qly, as 1., impaling, Qly, 1st and 4th, Gules a saltire argent (Nevile), 2nd, Argent a ship with three masts sails furled sable (   ), 3rd Gules fretty or (Audley)
Crest: As 1.
For Henry de Stafford O'Brien de Stafford, second son of Stafford O'Brien. He m. Lucy, dau. of the Rev. Henry William Nevile, of Walcot Park, co. Northampton, and d. 1880. (B.L.G. 7th ed.)

BOUGHTON HOUSE

1. All black background
On a lozenge   Qly, 1st, qly i & iv, qly France and England, ii, Scotland, iii, Ireland, over all a baton sinister argent, 2nd, qly i & iv, Argent three fusils conjoined in fess gules within a bordure sable (Montagu), ii & iii, Or an eagle displayed vert (Monthermer), 3rd, qly i & iv, Argent a human heart gules crowned with an imperial crown or, on a chief azure three molets argent (Douglas), ii & iii, Azure a bend between six cross crosslets fitchy or (Mar), all within a bordure or charged with a double tressure flory-counter-flory gules, 4th, Argent on a bend azure an estoile of six points between two crescents argent (Scott)   In pretence: Montagu quartering Monthermer

Duchess's coronet   Supporters: Dexter, A unicorn argent, maned and unguled or, gorged with a ducal coronet and chained or   Sinister, A griffin or langued gules, wings elevated and addorsed sable
Arms and supporters on a mantle gules and ermine
For Elizabeth, dau. of George, Duke of Montagu, who m. 1767, Henry, 3rd Duke of Buccleuch, K.G., and d. 21 Nov. 1827.   (B.P. 1949 ed.)
(An exact duplicate of this hatchment is in the possession of Mr. P.G. Summers, Day's Cottage, North Stoke, Oxford, which came originally from Buccleuch House, Richmond)

BRINGTON

1. Dexter background black
Qly argent and gules on the second and third quarters a fret or, over all on a bend sable three escallops argent (Spencer), impaling, Barry of eight or and gules (Poyntz)
Earl's coronet   Crest: Out of a ducal coronet or a griffin's head, wings expanded and elevated argent, gorged with a collar gemel gules
Mantling: Gules and ermine   Motto: Dieu defend le droit
Supporters: Dexter, A griffin wings elevated per fess ermine and or
Sinister, A wyvern wings elevated ermine   Each chained and gorged with a collar flory-counter-flory sable charged with three escallops argent
For John, 1st Earl Spencer, who m. 1755, Georgiana, dau. of Stephen Poyntz, of Midgham, co. Berks, and d. 31 Oct. 1783.   (B.P. 1928 ed.)

2. All black background
On a lozenge   Spencer impaling Poyntz   Countess's coronet
Motto and supporters, as 1. (but dexter supporter, per fess ermine and or ermined sable)
For Georgiana, widow of John, 1st Earl Spencer. She d. 18 Mar. 1814.

3. Sinister background black
Two shields   Dexter, within Garter, 1st and 4th Spencer, 2nd and 3rd, Churchill   Sinister, as dexter shield, impaling, Qly, 1st and 4th, Azure two bendlets between six crosses paty or (Bingham), 2nd and 3rd, Ermine a lion rampant gules (Turberville)
Countess's coronet   Supporters: As 2. (but both lined)
For Lavinia, dau. of Charles, 1st Earl of Lucan, who m. George John, 2nd Earl Spencer, and d. 8 June 1831.

4. All black background
Two shields   Dexter, within Garter, Spencer   Sinister, as dexter, impaling, Qly, 1st and 4th, Bingham, 2nd and 3rd, Turberville
Earl's coronet (above the crest, no helm)

Crest and motto, as 1.   Supporters, as 2.
Mantle: Gules and argent, on which is the Star of the Order of the
Garter   The George is shown beneath the shields suspended by the
Collar
For George John, 2nd Earl Spencer, who m. Lavinia, dau. of Charles,
1st Earl of Lucan, and d. 10 Nov. 1834.
(There is a duplicate of this hatchment in the church of St. Thomas,
Ryde, I.O.W.)

5. Sinister background black

Qly, 1st and 4th, Spencer, 2nd and 3rd, Sable a lion rampant argent, on
a canton argent a cross gules (Churchill)   In pretence: Qly, 1st and 4th,
Gules a maunch or between eight cinquefoils argent (Acklom), 2nd and
3rd, Qly ermine and gules (Stanhope)
Viscountess's coronet
Motto and supporters, as 2, (but sinister supporter lined, not chained)
On a mantle gules and ermine
For Esther, dau. and heiress of Richard Acklom, of Wiseton Hall, co.
Nottingham, who m. John Charles, Viscount Althorp (later 3rd Earl
Spencer), son of George John, 2nd Earl Spencer, and d. 11 June 1818.

6. All black background

Qly, 1st and 4th, Spencer, 2nd and 3rd, Churchill   In pretence: Qly,
1st and 4th, Acklom, 2nd and 3rd, Stanhope
Earl's coronet (above the crest)   Crest: As 1.
Motto and supporters, as 2. (but both lined, wyvern winged and bellied
gules with ermine spots)
On a mantle gules and argent
For John Charles, 3rd Earl Spencer, who m. Esther, dau. and heiress of
Richard Acklom and d. 1 Oct. 1845.

7. Sinister background black

Two shields   Dexter, within Garter, Spencer   Sinister, Spencer
In pretence: Qly, 1st and 4th, Barry of eight gules and or (Poyntz), 2nd
and 3rd, Sable three lions passant in bend between double cotises
argent (Brown)
Countess's coronet   Supporters, as 2.
For Elizabeth Georgiana, dau. of William Stephen Poyntz of Cowdray
House, Sussex, who m. as his 1st wife, Frederick, Viscount Althorp
(later 4th Earl Spencer) and d. 10 Apr. 1851.

8. Dexter background black

Two shields   Dexter, within Garter, Spencer   Sinister, Spencer
In pretence: Qly, 1st and 4th, Argent on a bend double cotised sable
three lions passant argent (Brown), 2nd and 3rd, Or three bars gules
(Poyntz) Also impaling, Qly, 1st and 4th, Sable on a bend cotised
argent a rose between two annulets gules (Conway), 2nd and 3rd, qly

i & iv, Or on a pile gules three lions passant guardant in pale or
between six fleurs-de-lys azure (Seymour), ii & iii, Gules two wings
conjoined in lure tips downwards or (Seymour)
The George is suspended between the shields   Earl's coronet
Crest and motto as 1., supporters, as 2.
For Frederick, 4th Earl Spencer, who m. 1st, Elizabeth Georgina, dau.
of William Stephen Poyntz, of Cowdray House, Sussex. She d. 10 Apr.
1851. He m. 2nd, Adelaide Horatia Elizabeth, dau. of Sir Horace
Beauchamp Seymour, and d. 27 Dec. 1857.

BROCKHALL

1. Dexter background black
Argent on a bend gules three escarbuncles of six points or (Thornton),
impaling, Gules a chevron vair between three roses argent (Reeve)
Crest: A demi-lion rampant argent
Mantling: Gules and argent   Motto: In coelo quies
Skull below shield
For Thomas Lee Thornton, who m. 1774, Mary, dau. of William Reeve,
and d. 22 Jan. 1790.   (B.L.G. 1937 ed.)

2. All black background
On a lozenge surmounted by three cherubs' heads
Thornton (escarbuncles of eight points), impaling, Reeve
Mantling: Gules and argent   Motto: Resurgam
For Mary, widow of Thomas Lee Thornton.   She d. 17 Feb. 1811.

3. Sinister background black
Qly, 1st and 4th, Thornton, as 2., 2nd and 3rd, Argent a fess between
three crescents sable (Lee)   In pretence: Qly, 1st and 4th, Azure
three sickles or (Fremeaux), 2nd and 3rd, Per pale azure and gules
three eagles displayed or (Cooke)
For Susanna, dau. and heiress of Peter John Fremeaux of Kingsthorpe,
who m. 1799, Thomas Reeve Thornton, son of Thomas Lee Thornton,
and d. 2 May 1846.

4. All black background
Qly, 1st and 4th, Thornton, 2nd and 3rd, Lee   In pretence: As 3.
Crest: A demi-lion rampant gules charged on the shoulder with an
escarbuncle or   Mantling: Gules and ermine   Motto: Resurgam
For Thomas Reeve Thornton, son of Thomas Lee Thornton. He m.
1799, Susanna, dau. and heiress of Peter John Fremeaux of
Kingsthorpe, and d. 25 Jan. 1862.

CANONS ASHBY

1. All black background
Azure a lion rampant and in chief a sphere between two estoiles or
(Dryden)
Crest: A demi-lion rampant azure holding in its dexter gamb a sphere or
Mantling: Gules and argent   Motto: in coelo salus
For Sir Robert Dryden, 3rd Bt., who d. unm. 19 Aug. 1708. (B.P.
1928 ed.)

2. Dexter background black
Dryden, impaling, Per fess gules and sable a chevron rompu between
three griffins' heads erased ermine (Allen)
Crest: As 1. but lion or   Mantling: Gules and argent   Motto: Mors
janua vitae
For Edward Dryden, who m. 1695, Elizabeth, dau. of Edward Allen of
Finchley, co. Middlesex, and d. 3 Nov. 1717.

3. All black background
Dryden, in dexter chief the Badge of Ulster, impaling, Argent two bars
gules (Martyn)
Crest: As 2.   Mantling: Gules and argent   Motto: Mors janua vitae
For Sir Erasmus Dryden, 6th Bt., who m. Elizabeth, dau. of Edward
Martyn of Westminster, and d. 3 Nov. 1718.

4. Sinister background black
Dryden, in dexter chief the Badge of Ulster   In pretence: Ermine on
a fess gules three escallops or (Ingram)
Motto: Mors janua vitae   Skull above shield
For Frances, dau. and heiress of Thomas Ingram of Barraby, co. Yorks,
who m. 1724, Sir John Dryden, 7th Bt., and d. Jan. 1724-5.

5. All black background
On a lozenge surmounted by a cherub's head
Dryden, in chief the Badge of Ulster, impaling, Sable an eagle close or
(Roper)
Motto: In coelo quies
For Elizabeth, dau. of John Roper, of Berkhamstead, co. Herts, who m.
as his second wife Sir John Dryden, 7th Bt. and d. 7 May 1791.

6. Dexter background black
Qly, 1st and 4th, Argent a millrind sable (Turner) in dexter chief of
the first quarter the Badge of Ulster, 2nd, Ermine on a chief dancetty
azure three griffins' heads erased or (Chaplin), 3rd, Azure a fess
indented between three martlets or (Page)   In pretence: Dryden
Crest: A lion passant guardant argent ducally crowned or holding in its
dexter paw a fer-de-moline sable

Mantling: Gules and argent   Motto: Resurgam
For John Turner (later Sir John Dryden, Bt.) who m. 1781, Elizabeth
dau. of Bevill Dryden, and in 1791 took the name and arms of Dryden
only. He was created a baronet in 1795, and d. 14 April, 1797. (Baker,
ii. 7)

7. All black background
Dryden, in dexter chief the Badge of Ulster
Crest: As 2.   Mantling: Gules and argent   Motto: Resurgam
For Sir John Edward Turner Dryden, 2nd Bt., who d. unm. 29 Sept.
1818.

8. Dexter background black
A plain shield and an ornamental lozenge
Shield   Azure on a bend argent three roundels azure a crescent for
cadency (Schooley)   In pretence: Dryden
Lozenge   Dryden, in chief the Badge of Ulster   In pretence: Dryden
Crest: Three garbs gules encircled by a coronet or
Mantling: Gules and argent   Motto: Esto memor brevis aevi
For Godfrey Schooley, of London, who m. as her second husband,
Elizabeth Dryden, and d. 4 Feb. 1819.

9. All black background
On a lozenge surmounted by a cherub's head
Dryden, in chief the Badge of Ulster   In pretence: Dryden
For Elizabeth, dau. of Bevill Dryden, of Marlborough, who m. 1st, John
Turner (later Sir John Dryden Bt.), who d. 1797, and 2nd, Godfrey
Schooley, and d. 5 Nov. 1824.

10.   Dexter background black
Dryden, in dexter chief the Badge of Ulster, impaling, Per pale gules and
azure a lion rampant argent between eight cross crosslets or (Hutchinson)
Crest: As 1.   No mantling or motto
For the Rev. Sir Henry Dryden, 3rd Bt. who m. Elizabeth, dau. of the
Rev. Julius Hutchinson, of Woodhall Park, co. Herts, and d. 17 Nov.
1837.

11. All black background
On a lozenge
Dryden impaling Hutchinson, as 10.
For Elizabeth, widow of the Rev. Sir Henry Dryden, 3rd Bt. She d. 22
Nov. 1851.

EAST CARLTON

1. All black background

Sable a chevron or between three crescents argent, in chief the Badge of
Ulster (Palmer)   In pretence: Ermine a griffin segreant gules (Grantham)
Crest: A wyvern or winged azure   Mantling: Gules and argent
Motto: Pr apprendre obleleis nepv
For Sir Geoffrey Palmer, 3rd Bt. who m. Elizabeth, dau. and co-heir of
Thomas Grantham of Goltho, co. Lincoln, and d. 29 Dec. 1732,
(B.P. 1949 ed.)

2. All black background

Palmer, in centre chief the Badge of Ulster, impaling, Argent a lion
rampant within a bordure engrailed sable (Harpur)
Crest: A wyvern or   Mantling: Gules and argent   Motto: Par sit
fortuna labori
Cherubs' heads at upper corners of shield and skull below
For Sir Thomas Palmer, 4th Bt., who m. Jemima, dau. of Sir John
Harpur, Bt. of Calke, co. Derby, and d. 14 June 1765.

3. Dexter background black

Palmer, impaling, Gules a fess wavy and in chief three piles also wavy
meeting in fess argent (Isham)
Crest: A wyvern or winged azure   Mantling: Gules and argent
Motto: Mors vitae initium   Skull in base
For Thomas Palmer of Carlton Curlieu, Leics, who m. 1793, Sophia,
dau. of Sir Justinian Isham, Bt. of Lamport, and d. 4 June 1810.

4. All black background

Palmer, impaling, Gules on a fess argent between three boars' heads
couped close or a lion passant azure (Gough) in centre chief (over both
coats) the Badge of Ulster
Crest: A wyvern or   Mantling: Gules and argent   Motto: Mors iter
ad vitam
Skull below
For Sir John Palmer, 5th Bt., who m. Charlotte, dau. of Sir Henry
Gough, Bt. of Edgbaston, co. Warwick, and d. 11 Feb. 1817.

5. All black background

Palmer, with Badge of Ulster on chevron, impaling, Argent on a
chevron engrailed azure between three martlets sable three crescents
or (Watson)
Crest: A wyvern or   Mantling: Argent (shaded)   Motto: Par sit
fortuna labori
For Sir John Henry Palmer, 7th Bt., who m. Mary Grace, dau. of
Lewis, 2nd Lord Sondes of Rockingham Castle, and d. 26 Aug. 1865.

6. All black background
Palmer, in centre chief the Badge of Ulster
Crest: A wyvern or   Mantling: Sable and or
Motto: Par sit fortuna labori
For Sir Geoffrey Palmer, 8th Bt., who d. unm. 10 Feb. 1892.

CATESBY

1. All black background
Argent a cross sable ermined argent between four stags trippant
proper (Parkhurst)
Crest: From a palisado crown or a buck's head argent attired or
Mantling: Gules and argent   Motto: Resurgam
Probably for Capt. John Parkhurst, who d. Dec. 1781. (Baker, i. 288)

2. Dexter background black
Ornamental shield with cherubs' heads at corners
Parkhurst   In pretence: Azure ten billets, four, three, two, one or,
from a chief or a lion issuant sable (Dormer)
Crest: From a palisado crown or a buck's head argent
Mantling: Gules and argent   Motto: In coelo quies
For John Parkhurst, who m. Ricarda, dau. and co-heiress of Robert
Dormer of Lee Grange, and d. Dec. 1765.   She d. Mar. 1770.

COURTEENHALL

1. All black background
On a lozenge   Qly, 1st and 4th, Argent two bars and in chief two
roundels gules (Wake), 2nd and 3rd, Argent on a chief vert a millpick
between two molets argent (Drury);   in chief the Badge of Ulster
In pretence: Argent a cross between four fleurs-de-lys sable (Fenton)
Motto: In coelo quies
For Mary, dau. and heiress of Richard Fenton, of Bank Top, co. York,
who m. 1765, Sir William Wake, 8th Bt. and d. 10 Dec. 1823.
(B.P. 1928 ed.)

2. All black background
Or two bars and in chief three roundels gules (Wake), impaling, two
coats per fess; in chief, Barry of eight or and vert three lions
rampant sable (Sitwell), and in base, Or ermined sable a fess wavy
azure between three Cornish choughs proper (Gambier)   In chief,
over line of impalement, the Badge of Ulster
Crest: The Wake knot or   Mantling: Gules and argent   Motto:
Resurgam
For Sir William Wake, 9th Bt. who m. 1st, Mary, dau. of Francis

Sitwell of Renishaw, co. Derby.   She d. 22 Nov. 1791. He m. 2nd,
Jenny, (d. 1837) dau. of Admiral James Gambier, and d. 27 Jan. 1846.

3. Dexter background black
Qly, 1st and 4th, Wake, 2nd and 3rd, Argent on a chief sable a cross
fitchy between two molets argent (Drury);   over all the Badge of
Ulster: impaling two coats per fess; in chief, Barry of eight or and
vert three lions rampant sable (Sitwell), and in base, Qly, 1st and 4th,
Argent a saltire engrailed and a chief gules (Tait), 2nd and 3rd, Or
two ravens hanging palewise sable with an arrow through both their
heads fesswise proper (Murdoch)
Crest: The Wake knot or   Mantling: Gules and argent
Motto: Vigila et ora
For Sir Charles Wake, 10th Bt. who m. 1st, Mary Alice, dau. of Sir
Sitwell Sitwell, Bt. of Renishaw.   She d.s.p. 1816.   He m. 2nd,
Charlotte Murdoch (d. 1888), dau. of Craufurd Tait, of Harviestown,
and d. 23 Feb. 1864.

4. Dexter background black
Wake, impaling, Qly ermine and or a bend engrailed gules surmounted
by another plain argent charged with three trefoils slipped sable
(Benson)   At honour point (over line of impalement) the Badge of
Ulster
Crest: The Wake knot or   Mantling: Gules and or
Motto: Vigila et ora
For Sir Hereward Wake, 13th Bt. who m. 1912, Margaret Winifred,
dau. of Robert Henry Benson of Buckhurst, Sussex, and d. 4 Aug.
1963.

DEENE

1. All black background
Qly, 1st and 4th, Or a saltire and a chief gules, on a canton argent a
lion rampant azure (Bruce), 2nd and 3rd, Argent a chevron gules
between three steel morions azure (Brudenell)
Crests: Dexter, A lion statant azure   Sinister, A sea horse argent
Mantling: Gules and or   Motto: En grace affie
Probably for James Ernest John Brudenell-Bruce, who d. unm. 11
Apr. 1917.

EASTON MAUDIT

1. All black background
Qly of nine, 1st, Argent three lions rampant and a chief gules
(Yelverton), 2nd, Gules a fess dancetty ermine between six cross

crosslets fitchy argent (Longueville), 3rd, Azure an eagle displayed
argent over all a bend gules (Wolverton), 4th, Gules three fish naiant in
pale argent (Roche), 5th, Barry of six argent and azure (Grey),
6th, Or a maunch gules (Hastings), 7th, Barry of ten argent and azure
eight martlets in orle gules (Valence), 8th, Gules on a saltire argent a
rose proper (Neville), 9th, Gules a lion rampant within a bordure
engrailed or (Talbot)
Earl's coronet   Crest: A lion statant reguardant gules
Mantling: Gules and ermine   Motto: Foy est tout   Supporters:
Dexter, A wyvern or gorged and lined gules   Sinister, A lion rampant
reguardant gules   Cherub's head in base
Probably for George Augustus, 2nd Earl of Sussex, d. unm. 8 Jan. 1758
(B.P. 1896 ed.)

2. Sinister background black
Yelverton, impaling, Argent a chevron engrailed between three talbots'
heads erased sable (Hall)
Countess's coronet   Mantle: Gules and ermine
Motto and supporters: As 1., but dexter, gorged and chained or
Cherub's head above coronet and skull in base
For Hester, dau. of John Hall, of Mansfield Woodhouse, co. Nottingham,
1st wife of Henry, 3rd Earl of Sussex.   She d. 11 Jan. 1777.

3. Sinister background black
Yelverton, impaling, Sable a chevron argent between three boys' heads
affronté couped at the shoulders proper, crined or, enwrapped about
the necks with a snake vert (Vaughan)
Countess's coronet   Motto: Foy en tout   Supporters: As 1., but
dexter lined gules
For Mary, dau. of John Vaughan of Bristol, 2nd wife of Henry, 3rd
Earl of Sussex.   She d. 17..

4. All black background
Yelverton impaling Vaughan, as 3.
Earl's coronet   Crest: As 1.   Mantling: Gules and argent
Motto and supporters: As 1., but dexter, gorged and lined gules
For Henry, 3rd Earl of Sussex, who m. 1st, Hester, dau. of John Hall,
and 2nd, Mary, dau. of John Vaughan, and d. 22 Apr. 1799.

EASTON NESTON

1. Dexter background black
Argent a cross patonce gules between four fleurs-de-lys vert, on a chief
azure a greyhound courant argent (Denys), impaling, Argent a fess
sable between three lions' heads erased gules (Fermor)
Crest: A demi-lion rampant or ermined sable collared gules holding a

spray of lilies in its dexter gamb proper
Mantling: Gules and argent   Motto: Hora e sempre
For Peter Denys, of the Pavilion, Chelsea, who m. 1787, Charlotte, only
dau. of George, 2nd Earl of Pomfret, and d. 27 June 1816. (Baker, ii, 144)

2. All black background
On a lozenge surmounted by a cherub's head
Denys impaling Fermor, as 1.
For Charlotte, widow of Peter Denys.   She d. Nov. 1835.

3. Dexter background black
Fermor, with crescent or for difference, impaling, Or in base a dolphin
naiant in waves of the sea proper, on a chief azure three molets argent
(Borough)
Earl's coronet   Crest: Out of a ducal coronet a cock's head gules combed
and wattled or   Motto: Hora e sempre   Supporters: Two lions
proper
Below the shield the Star of the Order of the Tower and Sword of
Portugal
For Thomas William, 4th Earl of Pomfret, who m. Amabel Elizabeth,
dau. of Sir Richard Borough, Bt., and d. 29 June 1833.

4. All black background
Fermor arms only
Earl's coronet   Crest, motto and supporters: As 3.
For George William Richard, 5th Earl of Pomfret, who d. unm. 8 June
1867.

5. Sinister background black
Argent a double-headed eagle displayed sable, in chief the Badge of
Ulster (Hesketh), impaling, Fermor
Shield suspended by a knot of blue ribbons and flanked by palm
branches
For Anna Maria Arabella, dau. of Thomas William, 4th Earl of Pomfret.
She m. 1846, Sir Thomas George Hesketh, Bt. and d. 25 Feb. 1870.

ECTON HALL

The two hatchments following were sold in 1956 and their present
whereabouts is unknown.
1. Dexter background black
Qly, 1st and 4th, Gules a chevron vair between three talbots' heads
erased or (Isted), 2nd and 3rd, Bendy lozengy or and sable a canton
ermine (Buck)   In pretence: Or a lion rampant azure (Percy)
Crests: Dexter, A buck's head erased attired and ducally gorged or

Sinister, A portcullis sable studded and chained or
Mantling: Gules and or   Motto: Nosce teipsum   Skull in base
For Samuel Isted, who m. Barbara, eldest dau. and co-heiress of
Thomas Percy, Bishop of Dromore, and d. 12 Aug. 1827.   (B.L.G.
7th ed.)

2. Sinister background black

Isted, impaling, Azure three lozenges, two and one, between eight cross
crosslets or (Stopford)
Shield surmounted with a cherub's head and flanked by palm branches
For Eleanor Elizabeth, dau. of the Hon. Rev. Richard Bruce Stopford.
She m. Ambrose, son of Samuel Isted, and d. 12 Oct. 1851.

EVERDON

1. All black background

Azure on a chevron or, between in chief two doves argent and in base
an anchor erect or, three roses gules barbed proper (Doveton)
Crest: A dove, wings displayed argent, supporting with its dexter claw
a staff with a pennon (hoist, cross of St. George; fly, red white and
blue, lengthwise)
Mantling: Gules and ermine   Motto: Patience and perseverance
For General Gabriel Doveton, d. May 1824.   (Baker, i. 365)

FAWSLEY

1. Dexter background black

Qly, 1st and 4th, Ermine, 2nd and 3rd, Paly of six or and gules
(Knightley)   In pretence: Argent on a chevron between three goats'
heads erased sable three escallops argent (Benson) Also impaling,
Ermine three cats passant guardant in pale tails coward azure (Adams)
Crest: A buck's head couped argent attired or   Mantling: Gules and
argent
For Lucy Knightley, who m. 1st, Jane Grey, dau. and co-heir of Henry
Benson, of Dodford, co. Northampton.   She d. 3 Dec. 1731.   He m.
2nd, 1732, Anne, dau. of the Rev. William Adams, Rector of
Charwelton, and d. 20 Aug. 1738.   (Baker, i. 383)

2. All black background

On a lozenge surmounted by a cherub's head
Knightley, impaling, Argent on a fess double cotised gules three
griffins' heads erased or (Dashwood)
Motto: Resurgam
For Catherine, dau. of Sir James Dashwood, Bt., of Kirtlington Park,
co. Oxford, who m. Lucy Knightley, of Fawsley, and d. 27 June 1809.

(B.P. 1928 ed.)

3. All black background
Knightley, at fess point the Badge of Ulster, impaling, Gules on a bend
argent three trefoils slipped vert (Hervey)
Crest: A buck's head couped argent attired or
Mantling: Gules and argent   Motto: Envita fortuna
For Sir Charles Knightley, 2nd Bt. who m. Selina Mary, dau of Felton
Lionel Hervey, and d. 30 Aug. 1864.   (B.P. 1928 ed.)

GRENDON

1. All black background
Sable a lion passant guardant or between three esquires' helmets argent
(Compton), impaling, Qly, 1st and 4th, Argent on a cross gules a crown
or (Nicholas), 2nd and 3rd, Argent a fess wavy sable between three
ravens proper (Nicholas)
Crest: On a mount a beacon fired proper and a ribbon inscribed with
the words 'Nisi Dominus'
Mantling: Gules and argent   Motto: Ie ne serchs que ung
For Hatton Compton, who m. Penelope, dau. of Sir John Nicholas, and
d. 1740.   (Markham)

2. All black background
Compton, on a crescent argent a crescent sable for difference
Crest: As 1.   Mantling: Gules and argent   Motto: In coelo quies
Skull in base
Unidentified

3. Dexter background black
Compton, a molet for difference, impaling, Argent a chevron potent
ringed at the point between three crescents sable (Walker)
Crest: As 1.   Mantling: Gules and argent.   Motto: In coelo
quies
Cherubs' heads at corners of shield
Unidentified

WEST HADDON

1. All black background
Gules two bars argent, over all on a bend or a roundel gules between
two leopards' faces azure, a martlet or for cadency (Heygate), impaling,
Azure a crescent argent between three fleurs-de-lys or, within a
bordure engrailed argent (Unwin)
Crest: A wolf's head erased gules langued argent, charged with a martlet

or for cadency   Mantling: Gules and argent   Motto: Resurgam
For James Heygate, fourth surviving son of Nicholas Heygate; he m.
1781, Sarah, dau. of Samuel Unwin of Hackney, Middlesex, and d. 1833
(Markham)

HARDINGSTON

1. All black background

Qly, 1st and 4th, Per fess or and argent a double-headed eagle displayed
sable, on the breast an escutcheon gules charged with a bend vair
(Bouverie), 2nd and 3rd, Argent on a bend gules between three
roundels sable three swans rising or, on a sinister canton azure a demi-
horse salient argent charged with a dexter baton gules in chief two
pheons or (Clarke), in centre chief a label of three points sable
In pretence: Qly, 1st and 4th, Argent two chevronels between three
castle gules (Castle), 2nd and 3rd, Argent on a chevron sable between
three Cornish choughs proper three leopards' faces or (   )
Crest: A demi-eagle with two heads displayed sable ducally gorged or,
on the breast a cross crosslet argent
Mantling: Gules and argent   Motto: Patria cara carior libertas
For Edward Bouverie, who m. 1788, Catherine, only dau. and heiress
of William Castle, and d. 14 April 1858. (B.L.G. 1886 ed)

2. Dexter background black

Qly, 1st and 4th, qly i & iv, Bouverie, ii & iii, Argent on a bend gules
between two roundels sable three swans' wings close or, on a sinister
canton azure a demi-ram salient between three fleurs-de-lys a dexter
baton argent (Clarke), 2nd and 3rd, qly i & iv, Argent two chevronels
between three billets sable (   ), ii & iii, Argent on a chevron gules
between three martlets sable three bezants (   ), impaling, Or issuant
from the dexter a cubit sinister arm, vested azure, cuffed argent,
grasping a cross crosslet fitchy gules (O'Donel)
Crest and motto: As 1. Shield flanked by flags, to the dexter, white,
red and blue, and to the sinister, green, blue and red
For General Éverard William Bouverie, who m. 1816, Charlotte, dau.
of Colonel Hugh O'Donel, of Newport Pratt, co. Mayo, and d. 18 Nov.
1871.

3. Dexter background black

Sable a cross moline between four escallops or (Vade), impaling, Or on
a fess between two chevrons sable three cross crosslets or (Walpole)
Crest: A dexter arm in armour embowed sable garnished or the hand
grasping a dagger point downwards proper
Mantling: Gules and or   Motto: In coelo quies
For the Rev. Ashton Vade, Vicar of Hardingston, who m. Mary

Rachael, dau. of the Hon. Richard Walpole, and d. 26 May 1820.
(Mon. in church)

HARLESTON

1. All black background
Gules on a saltire or another saltire vert (Andrew), impaling, Argent on
a bend gules three molets of eight points or (Thornton)
Crest: A Moor's head in profile couped at the shoulders proper,
filleted or and gules   Mantling: Gules and argent
Motto: Resurgam   Cherubs' heads at upper angles of shield
For Robert Andrew, who m. 1763, Frances, (d. 1799) dau. of Thomas
Thornton, of Brockhall, and d. 20 Apr. 1807.   (Baker, i. 168)

2. All black background
Andrew, impaling, Qly sable and or the first and fourth quarters
charged with a cinquefoil ermine (Packe)
Crest: A Moor's head in profile couped at the neck proper
Mottoes: Above crest, Crux et praesidium et decum   Below shield,
Resurgam
For Robert Andrew, who m. 1799, Frances, dau. of James Packe, of
Prestwold, co. Leicester, and d. 5 Aug. 1832.

HARRINGWORTH

1. Dexter background black
Azure a fess crenelly between three estoiles of six points or (Tryon),
impaling, Argent two bars sable (Brereton)
Crest: A bear's head sable semy of estoiles or
No mantling or motto
For Thomas Tryon, who m. Harriet, dau. of the Rev. William Brereton,
and d. 29 June 1825.   (B.L.G. 7th ed.)

HARROWDEN HALL

1. All black background
On a lozenge surrounded by ornamental scrollwork
Qly, 1st and 4th, Argent on a chevron engrailed azure between three
martlets sable three crescents or (Watson), 2nd and 3rd, Sable a
chevron between three leopards faces or (Wentworth) In pretence:
Ermine on a fess gules a lion passant or (Proby)
For Alice, dau. of Sir Thomas Proby, Bt. of Elton, who m. the Hon.
Thomas Watson-Wentworth, of Harrowden, and d. 1743.   (B.E.B.)

HASELBEACH

1. Three-quarters background black
Shield and lozenge joined by a knot of ribbon
Shield   Sable a bend between six escallops or (Foljambe), impaling,
Per pale or and sable a chevron between three horses bits counterchanged
(Milner)   Also, in pretence: Qly, 1st, Azure on a fess wavy argent a
cross formy gules in chief two estoiles of six points or, on a chief wavy
argent a cormorant sable in its beak a branch of laver vert (Jenkinson),
2nd, Sable a chevron between three molets argent (Shuckburgh), 3rd,
Azure a griffin passant or, a chief or (Evelyn), 4th, Argent two bars
gemel sable in chief three molets pierced sable (Medley)
Crest: A leg couped at the thigh qly or and sable spurred or
Mantling: Sable and or   Motto: Soyez ferme
Supporters: Dexter, An antelope qly or and sable.   Sinister, A lion
argent ducally gorged and lined or
Lozenge, ensigned with a viscount's coronet
Qly, 1st and 4th, Lozengy argent and gules (Fitzwilliam), 2nd and
3rd, Sable a chevron between three leopards' faces or (Wentworth)
In pretence: As on dexter shield
Supporters: Two wild men wreathed about the loins and temples with
leaves, the outer arms embowed, each holding across the body a tree
eradicated, the top broken proper
For George Savile Foljambe, who m. 1st, 1828, Harriet Emily Mary,
dau. of Sir William Mordaunt Sturt Milner, Bt., and 2nd, Selina
Charlotte, dau. of Charles, 3rd Earl of Liverpool, and widow of
Viscount Milton, and d. 18 Dec. 1869.   (B.L.G. 1886 ed.)

HORTON

1. All black background
On a shield, surrounded with the collar of the Order of the Bath,
Gules on a fess ermine between three doves proper three crosses formy
gules, in centre chief the Badge of Ulster (Gunning)
Crest: A dove argent holding in its dexter claw a caduceus proper
Mantling: Gules and argent   Motto: Imperis regit unus aequo
Supporters: Dexter, A stag proper gorged with a collar dancetty argent
and gules   Sinister, A fox proper gorged with a collar dancetty
argent and gules
For Sir Robert Gunning, K.B., 1st Bt., who m. Anne, dau. of Robert
Sutton of Scofton, Notts, and d. 22 Sept. 1816.   (B.P. 1928 ed.)

LAMPORT

1. All black background
Gules a fess wavy and in chief three piles also wavy points meeting in
fess argent, on the fess the Badge of Ulster (Isham)
Crest: A demi-swan with wings displayed argent
Mantling: Gules and argent   Motto: Resurgam   Cherub's head in
base   (Restored 1954 by C.B. Savage)
For Sir Justinian Vere Isham, 9th Bt., who d. unm. 25 Aug. 1846.
(B.P. 1949 ed.)

LICHBOROUGH

1. All black background
Gules a fess dancetty ermine between three eastern crowns or (Grant)
Crest: On a burning mount a cross issuing flames proper
Mantling: Gules and ermine   Motto: (in front of crest) Stand sure
For William Grant, who d. unm. 1840. (B.L.G. 1937 ed.)

2. All black background
On a lozenge   Grant, impaling, Argent a chevron between three
Moors' heads couped sable (Ives)
For Ann, dau. of William Ives, of Bradden, who m. Thomas Grant and
d. 1849.

3. Dexter background black
Grant, impaling, Gules three cinquefoils argent, on a chief ermine a
cornucopia surmounting a caduceus in saltire proper (Pack)
Crest: As 1. (with motto above)   Mantling: Gules and argent
Motto: In coelo quies
For William Grant, who m. Frances Simpson, dau. of Richard Pack,
of Flore House, co. Northampton, and d. 18 July 1868.

LOIS WEEDON

1. All black background
Sable a chevron between three griffins' heads erased argent, on a chief
or a lion passant between two roundels gules (Jennens)
Crest: A leopard's head erased gules bezanty holding in its mouth a
cross formy fitchy bendwise argent
Mantling: Gules and or   Motto: Mors janua vitae
For Richard Jennens, who d. unm. 3 March 1773.   (Baker, i. 720
& ii. 113)

2. All black background
On a lozenge surrounded by ornamental gold scrollwork and
surmounted by a cherub's head
Per fess sable and gules a lion rampant or holding in its dexter gamb a
cinquefoil slipped argent (Heber)
Motto: In coelo quies
For Mary Heber, who d. unm. 2 Sept. 1809.   (Baker i. 720)

3. Dexter background black
Qly, 1st, Argent a human heart gules crowned with an imperial crown
or, on a chief azure three molets argent, all within a bordure argent
charged with eight oak leaves proper (Douglas), 2nd, Argent a cross
counter-embattled sable (Auchinleck), 3rd, Argent on a chief gules
three pales or (Keith), 4th, Azure three boars' heads couped within
a bordure or (Gordon), impaling, Qly, 1st and 4th, Or a fess counter-
compony argent and gules between three griffins' heads erased gules
(Wrightson), 2nd and 3rd, Per fess gules and sable a lion rampant or,
in dexter chief an estoile of six points or (Heber)
Crest: A demi-wildman holding over his right shoulder a club,
wreathed about the loins and temples proper; above the crest on a
scroll the motto 'Jamais arriere'   Motto (below shield): In coelo quies
Supporters: Two wild men wreathed about the loins and temples proper
The dexter supporter has pendent from his free hand a shield bearing
the arms: Argent a human heart gules crowned with an imperial crown
or, on a chief azure three molets argent (Douglas)   The sinister supporter
has pendent from his free hand a shield bearing the arms: Azure a
lion passant or between three fleurs-de-lys argent (North)
(Restored by C.B. Savage, 1955)
For the Hon. Frederick Sylvester North Douglas, who m. Harriet, dau.
of William Wrightson, of Cusworth, Yorkshire, and d. 21 Oct. 1819.
(B.E.P.)

LOWICK

1. All black background
Within the Garter, Qly or and gules over all a bend vair (Sackville)
Duke's coronet   Crest: Out of a coronet of fleurs-de-lys or an estoile
of eight points argent   Mantle: Gules and ermine   Motto: Aut
nunquam tentes aut perfice   Supporters: Two leopards argent
spotted sable
For Charles Sackville Germain, 5th Duke of Dorset, K.G., d. unm. 29
July 1843. (B.E.P.)

2. Dexter background black
Qly, 1st and 4th, Qly or and gules a bend vair surmounted by a canton
ermine, a crescent sable for cadency (Sackville), 2nd and 3rd, Azure

three lozenges, two and one, between nine cross crosslets or (Stopford)
In pretence: Sackville (no canton)
Crests: Dexter, Out of a coronet of fleurs-de-lys or, charged with a
trefoil slipped argent, an estoile of six points argent charged with a
crescent sable   Sinister, A wyvern proper   Mantling: Gules and
argent   Motto: Tous jours loyal
For William Bruce Stopford, of Drayton House, Northamptonshire, who
m. 1837 , Caroline Harriet, dau. of the Hon. George Germain, and d. 29
Apr. 1872.   (B.E.P.)

MARSTON TRUSSEL

1. Dexter background black
Argent three martlets sable between two bars gules (Barwell), impaling,
Per pale gules and azure a lion rampant ermine (Norwich)
Crest: A dolphin naiant embowed proper   Mantling: Gules and argent
For Henry Barwell, who m. Arabella Catherine, dau. of Sir Erasmus
Norwich, Bt. and d. 24 Apr. 1763. (Wotton's Baronetage, ii. 214)

MIDDLETON CHENEY

1. Dexter background black
Sable a stag's head cabossed argent attired or (Horton), impaling, Per
pale or and gules a chevron between three molets all counterchanged
(Sufflé)
Crest: On waves of the sea proper a dolphin naiant or enfiled on a spear
palewise point upwards proper   Mantling: Gules and argent
Motto: Resurgam
For William Horton, who m. Elizabeth, dau. and heiress of Petter Sufflé,
of Middlesex, and d. 23 Sept. 1833.   (B.L.G. 7th ed. Date from
gravestone)

2. All black background
On a lozenge surrounded by decorative scrollwork and surmounted by
a cherub's head   Horton impaling Sufflé
Motto: Resurgam
For Elizabeth, widow of William Horton.   She d. 25 Sept. 1833.
(Date from gravestone)

3. All black background
Sable a stag's head cabossed argent attired or (Horton)
Crest, mantling and motto: As 1.
Probably for a son of William and Elizabeth Horton.

4. All black background
On a lozenge
Qly, 1st and 4th, Per fess azure and sable a stag's head cabossed argent
in chief three roses argent (Horton), 2nd and 3rd, Per pale or and gules
a chevron indented between in chief two molets and in base a mascle
all counterchanged (Sufflé)
For Mary Ann, dau. of William and Elizabeth Horton.   She d. 1869.
(Date from gravestone)

NORTON

1. All black background
On a lozenge surmounted by a cherub's head
Azure a bend between six molets or (Breton), impaling, Or on a chief
indented sable three crescents argent (Harvey)
For Mary, dau. of Edward Harvey, of Combe Nevill, Surrey, who m.
1707, Nicholas Breton, and d. May 1764.   He d. 23 Sept. 1716.
(Baker, i. 417)

2. Dexter background black
Azure a bend between six molets pierced or (Breton)   In pretence:
Qly, 1st and 4th, Azure a lion passant between three pheons or
(Wolstenholme), 2nd and 3rd, Sable two chevronels between three
molets or (Rainton)
Crest: A lion's gamb erased or
Mantling: Gules and argent   Motto: In coelo quies
For Eliab Breton, son of Nicholas Breton, who m. Elizabeth, dau. and
co-heir of Sir William Wolstenholme, Bt. of Enfield, Middlesex, and d.
19 Dec. 1785.

3. Dexter background black
Azure a bend between six molets or (Breton), impaling, Vert a chevron
between three crescents argent (Martin)
Crest: A lion's gamb erased or charged with three billets sable
Mantling: Gules and argent   Motto: In coelo quies
For Michael Harvey Breton, eldest son of Eliab Breton, who m. Agnes,
dau. of John Martin, and d. 18 June 1798.

4. Dexter background black
Barry of twelve or and sable (Botfield), impaling, Azure on a bend
argent between six lozenges or a cross formy gules (Withering)
Crest: A reindeer statant or   Mantling: Gules and argent
Motto: Resurgam
For Beriah Botfield, who m. 1806, Charlotte, dau. of William Withering,
and d. 27 Apr. 1813.   (B.L.G. 6th ed.)

5. All black background
On a lozenge surmounted by a cherub's head
Barry of twelve sable and or (Botfield), impaling, Azure on a bend
argent between six lozenges or a cross formy gules (Withering)
For Charlotte, dau. of William Withering, widow of Beriah Botfield.
She d. 1825.

6. Dexter background black
Barry of twelve or and sable (Botfield), impaling, Qly per fess indented
or and gules (Leighton)
Crest: A reindeer statant or   Mantling: Sable and or
Motto: J'ay bonne cause
For Beriah Botfield, son of Beriah Botfield, who m. Isabella, dau. of
Sir Baldwin Leighton, Bt. of Loton Park, Shrewsbury, and d. 7 Aug.
1863.

GREAT OAKLEY

1. Sinister background black (dexter ermine)
Or an anchor azure, on a chief azure three arming buckles or (Supple)
In pretence: Or on a fess azure three escallops or (Brooke)
Crest: A demi sea horse argent   Motto: Mors janua vitae
Probably for Mary, eldest dau. and heiress of Arthur Brooke, who m.
Richard Supple, of Aghadoe, co. Cork, and d. 1782.   (B.P. 1928 ed.)

2. All black background
On a lozenge surmounted by a cherub's head
Supple   In pretence: Brooke   Also impaling two coats per pale:
dexter, Supple, sinister, Gules seven mascles three, three and one or
(Quincy) both within a bordure argent
Motto: Melior resurgam   Skull in base
For Anna Quincy, 2nd wife of Richard Supple.   She d. 18..

3. Dexter background black
Qly, 1st and 4th, Brooke with Badge of Ulster in dexter chief of first
quarter, 2nd and 3rd, Supple   In pretence: Argent two bars and in
chief three lions' heads erased gules (Worge)
Crests: Dexter, A demi sea horse argent finned and maned or
Sinister, A dexter cubit arm in armour proper, the hand grasping an
anchor flukes upwards azure (Supple)
Mantling: Gules and argent   Motto: Spes mea Deus
For Sir Richard de Capell Brooke, Bt., son of Richard Supple, by Mary
Brooke, the heiress of Oakley. In 1788, he m. Mary, only dau. and
heiress of Major-General Worge, of Sussex, and in 1797, he assumed
the names of de Capell and Brooke. In 1803 he was created a baronet,
and d. 27 Nov. 1829.

4. Dexter background black

Qly, as last, with Badge of Ulster, impaling, Argent a chevron sable
between three lions' heads erased gules langued sable (Johnson)
Crests: As 3.   Mantling: Gules and argent   Motto: Spes mea Deus
For Sir Arthur de Capell Brooke, 2nd Bt., who m. Elizabeth
Johnson, widow of J.J. Eyre.   He d.s.p. 6 Dec. 1858.

5. All black background

Qly, as last, with Badge of Ulster, over all a crescent gules for cadency
Crest: A demi sea-horse argent finned and maned or
Mantling: Gules and argent   Motto: Spes mea Deus
For Sir Edward Geoffrey de Capell Brooke, 6th Bt., who d. unm. 6 Oct.
1968.

PAULERSPURY

The three following hatchments have disappeared and were probably
destroyed 1968/9.

1. Dexter background black

Azure on a chevron between three griffins' heads erased argent three
cross crosslets gules, on a chief argent an escallop azure between two
cinquefoils gules (Shedden), impaling, Gules crusilly a lion rampant or
(Goodrich)
Crest: A hermit couped at the shoulders proper vested russet
Mantling: Gules and argent   Motto: indecipherable
For Robert Shedden, who m. 1767, in Virginia, Agatha, dau. of John
Goodrich of Nansemond Plantation, and d. 29 Sept. 1826.   (B.L.G.
3rd ed.)

2. All black background

On an ornamental lozenge surmounted by a cherub's head and flanked
by palm branches
Shedden impaling Goodrich (but cross crosslets fitchy on Shedden coat)
Motto: Resurgam
For Agatha, widow of Robert Shedden.   She d. 1837.

3. Sinister background black

On a shield surmounted by a cherub's head
Shedden with Goodrich in pretence
For Mary, dau. and co-heiress of William Goodrich of Spring Hill,
I.O.W., who m. George, eldest son of Robert and Agatha Shedden, and
d. 2 Dec. 1827.

POLEBROOK

1. Dexter background black

Qly, 1st and 4th, Azure a buckle argent between three boars' heads couped or (Ferguson), 2nd and 3rd, Vert a fleur-de-lys or between two molets in fess argent, in chief two roses argent and in base three arrows points downwards palewise in fess or tipped and flighted argent (   ), impaling, Or ermined sable, on a mount vert a greyhound passant sable (Holforth)
Crest: A thistle proper   Mantling: Vert and argent
Motto: Dulcius ex asperis
For Col. John Stevenson Ferguson, who m. 1863, Sophia Jane Holforth, of Rusholme Hall, and d. 11 Jan. 1885.   (B.L.G. 1937 ed.)

PRESTON DEANERY

1. Dexter background black

Qly, 1st and 4th, Azure a lamb passant proper bearing over the sinister shoulder a staff with a pennon gules, on a chief or a tower of two turrets between two gabions proper (Christie), 2nd and 3rd, Argent three bears' heads erased sable muzzled or, a martlet for cadency (Langham), impaling, Qly, 1st and 4th, Gules a chevron between three crescents or (Gosling), 2nd and 3rd, Sable three conies courant argent (Cunliffe)
Crest: A brown bear passant muzzled and chained or, the chain reflexed over the shoulder; on the flank a roundel sable charged with a cross argent, the dexter paw resting on an escutcheon per pale or and sable
Mantling: Gules and argent   Motto: In coelo quies
For Langham Christie, who m. Margaret Elizabeth, dau. of William Gosling of Hassobury Park, Essex, and d. 23 Sept. 1861.   (B.L.G. 1932 ed.)

2. All black background

On a lozenge flanked by cherubs' heads
Christie impaling Gosling
Motto: Resurgam
For Margaret Elizabeth, widow of Langham Christie.   She d. 14 Dec. 1866.

RAVENSTHORP

1. All black background

Qly sable and or a bend argent (Langton), impaling, Argent on a cross sable five bezants (Stratton)
Crest: Two winged serpents interwoven and erect on their tails vert

Mantling: Gules and argent   Motto: (painted out)
For Thomas Langton of Teeton Hall, who m. Elizabeth, dau. of Stratton
Stratton, of London, and d. 21 Aug. 1762.   (Baker, i. 221)

2. Dexter background black
Langton, with impalement uncharged
Crest: As 1.   Mantling: Gules and argent   Motto: Resurgam
Probably for Thomas Langton, only son of Thomas and Elizabeth
Langton. He m. Susannah, dau. of Joseph Basset, and d. 28 May 1801.

ROTHWELL

1. Dexter background black
Sable a stag trippant a chief indented or, in chief the Badge of Ulster
(Humble), impaling, Azure three sinister gauntlets or (Vane)
Crest: A demi-stag salient or gorged with a chaplet of laurel proper
Mantling: Gules and argent
For Sir William Humble, Bt., who m. 1732, Elizabeth, dau. of Gilbert,
Lord Barnard, of Barnard Castle, co. Durham, and d. 1742. (B.E.B. &
Wotton)

2. All black background
On a lozenge   Humble impaling Vane, as 1.
Motto: In coelo quies
For Elizabeth, Lady Humble, d. Feb. 1770.

3. Sinister background black
On a shield suspended by a knot of ribbons, with cherubs' heads at
upper angles
Qly, 1st, Gules a chevron ermine between three garbs or (Hill), 2nd,
Paly of six azure and gules, on a chief azure a lion passant or
(Loddington), 3rd, Ermine a lion rampant sable (Lambe), 4th, Argent
a chevron between three maunches sable (Maunsell)   In pretence:
Qly per fess indented gules and azure three lions rampant argent
(Medlycott)
Motto: Resurgam
For Ann Barbara, dau. and heiress of Thomas Medlycott, of
Cottingham, who m. George Hill of Rothwell, and d. 10 Aug. 1800.
(Markham)

4. All black background
Qly, as 2. with Medlycott in pretence
Crest: A dove rising argent in the beak an olive branch proper
Mantling: Gules and argent   Motto: Resurgam
For George Medlycott (formerly Hill) who m. Ann Barbara, dau. and
heiress of Thomas Medlycott, of Cottingham. He took the name and
arms of Medlycott, and d. 21 Feb. 1808.

5. All black background
On a lozenge suspended by knots of ribbons
Qly, 1st and 4th, Argent three cocks gules beaked, combed and wattled
sable (Cockayne), 2nd and 3rd, Gules three lions passant guardant per
pale or and argent (O'Brien)   In pretence: Qly, 1st and 4th, Qly per
fess indented gules and azure three lions passant guardant argent
(Medlycott), 2nd and 3rd, Gules a chevron ermine between three garbs or
(Hill)
For Barbara, dau. of George Medlycott (formerly Hill), who m. the Hon.
William Cockayne, of Rushton Hall, and d. 21 June 1838.

RUSHTON MANOR

1. Sinister background black
Qly, 1st and 4th, Gules four bars and a chief argent, a canton gules for
difference (Thornhill), 2nd and 3rd, Or a cross raguly between four
trefoils slipped vert (Clarke)   In pretence: Thornhill (no canton)
For Clara Capel Clarke-Thornhill, dau. and co-heiress of Thomas
Thornhill of Fixey Hall, Yorks, who m. William Capel Clarke (who
took his wife's name and arms on his marriage) and d. 16 July 1865.
(B.L.G. 7th ed.)

STAMFORD BARON

1. Dexter background black
Two shields   Dexter, within Garter, and the George pendent, Barry
of ten argent and azure six escutcheons sable each charged with a
lion rampant argent (Cecil)   Sinister, within ornamental wreath,
Cecil, and in pretence: Barry of eight or and gules (Poyntz)
Marquess' coronet   Crest: On a chapeau gules and ermine a garb or
supported by two lions, the dexter argent, the sinister azure
Motto: Cor unum via una   Supporters: Two lions ermine langued
gules
For Brownlow, 2nd Marquess of Exeter, K.G., who m. 1824, Isabella,
dau. of William Stephen Poyntz, of Cowdray House, Sussex, and d.
16 Jan. 1867.   (B.P. 1928 ed.)

2. All black background
A shield and a lozenge   Dexter (shield), within Garter, Cecil
Sinister (lozenge), Cecil   In pretence: Poyntz (gules and or)
Marchioness's coronet   Supporters: Two lions ermine
For Isabella, dau. of William Stephen Poyntz, and widow of Brownlow,
2nd Marquess of Exeter.   She d. 6 March 1879.

3. Dexter background black
Cecil, impaling, Qly, 1st, Qly or and gules in the first quarter an eagle
displayed vert (Pakenham), 2nd, Argent on a bend indented sable
between two cotises azure each charged with three bezants three fleurs-
de-lys argent (Cuffe), 3rd, Ermine a griffin segreant azure (Aungier),
4th, Per bend embattled argent and gules (Boyle)
Crest, motto and supporters: As 1.
For William Alleyne, 3rd Marquess of Exeter, who m. Georgiana Sophia,
dau. of Thomas 1st Earl of Longford, and d. 14 July 1895.

4. Dexter background black
Cecil   In pretence: Ermine two boars passant gules (Whichcote)
Marquess' coronet   Crest, motto and supporters: As 1.
For Brownlow Henry George, 4th Marquess of Exeter, who m. 1875,
Isabella, dau. and heiress of Sir Thomas Whichcote, Bt., and d. 9 Apr.
1898.

STANFORD

1. All black background
Azure fretty argent, in dexter chief the Badge of Ulster (Cave)
In pretence: Or a chevron engrailed barry wavy azure and argent
between three cranes azure (Browne)   In a square to dexter of main
shield, Cave impaling Browne: all black background   In a square to
sinister of main shield, Cave, impaling, Qly per fess indented gules and
or, on an escutcheon argent a griffin segreant vert (Bromley): dexter
background black
Crest: A greyhound courant sable   Mantling: Gules and argent
Motto: Gardez   At base of frame is the date 1703
For Sir Roger Cave, 2nd Bt., who m. 1st, Martha, dau. and heir of John
Browne of Eydon, co. Northampton, and 2nd, Mary, dau. of Sir William
Bromley, of Baginton, co. Warwick, and d. 11 Oct. 1703.
(B.P. 1928 ed.)

2. Dexter background black
Cave, in dexter chief the Badge of Ulster, impaling, Azure on a cross
argent five molets gules (Verney)
Crest: A greyhound courant sable   Mantling: Gules and argent
Frame decorated with skulls and crossbones, in the lower angle 1719.
For Sir Thomas Cave, 3rd Bt., who m. Margaret, dau. of John, Viscount
Fermanagh, of Claydon, Bucks, and d. 21 Apr. 1719.

3. All black background
On an ornamental lozenge
Cave, in fess point the Badge of Ulster, impaling Verney
Motto: In coelo quies (all of motto except quies missing)

On lower angle of frame the words: Cave   Beware
For Margaret, widow of Sir Thomas Cave, 3rd Bt.   She d. 17 May
1774.

4. All black background
Cave, in dexter chief the Badge of Ulster
Crest: A greyhound courant sable collared argent, on a scroll above the
motto 'Gardes'   Mantling: Gules and argent   Motto: Mors mihi
lucrum   Date on base of frame, 1734
For Sir Verney Cave, 4th Bt., d. unm. 13 Sept. 1734.

5. Sinister background black
Cave, impaling, Qly per fess indented azure and argent in the first
quarter a lion passant guardant (? Croft) N.B. Lion almost
indistinguishable.
Crest: A greyhound courant sable collared argent
Mantling: Gules and argent   Motto: Gardez
Unidentified

6. All black background
Cave, in chief the Badge of Ulster   In pretence: Or a chevron
between three molets pierced sable (Davies)
Crest: A greyhound courant sable collared argent, on a scroll above the
motto 'Gardes'   Mantling: Gules and argent   Motto: In coelo quies
Skull in base
For Sir Thomas Cave, 5th Bt., who m. Elizabeth, only dau. and heir of
Griffith Davies, of Birmingham, and d. 7 Aug. 1778.

7. Dexter background black
Qly, 1st and 4th, Cave, in dexter chief of first quarter the Badge of
Ulster, 2nd and 3rd, Davies   In pretence: Per bend sinister ermine and
sable ermined argent a lion rampant crowned or armed and langued
gules (Edwards)
Crest: A greyhound courant sable, on a scroll above the motto 'Gardez'
Mantling: Gules and argent   Motto: In coelo quies
Skull in base
For Sir Thomas Cave, 6th Bt., who m. Sarah, dau. of John Edwards, of
London, and d. 30 May 1780.

8. All black background
On a lozenge surmounted by a cherub's head
Qly, 1st and 4th, Cave, 2nd and 3rd, Or a chevron between three molets
sable (Davies) in chief the Badge of Ulster   In pretence: Per bend sable
ermined or and ermine a lion rampant crowned or (Edwards)
Motto: In coelo quies
For Sarah, widow of Sir Thomas Cave, 6th Bt. She d. July 1819.

9. Dexter background black

Cave, impaling, Argent a chevron between three roundels gules
(Sherard)
Crest: A greyhound courant sable holding in its mouth a scroll with the
motto 'Gardes'   Mantling: Gules and argent
Motto: Mors janua vitae   Shield edged with leaves, skull below
For Sir Thomas Cave, 7th Bt., who m. Lucy, dau. of Robert, 4th Earl
of Harborough, and d. 15 Jan. 1792.

10. Dexter background black

Argent a pile sable a chevron counterchanged (Otway)
In pretence: Cave
Crest: Out of a ducal coronet or two wings expanded sable
Mantling: Gules and argent   Motto: Si deus nobiscum quis contra nos
For Henry Otway, of Castle Otway, co. Tipperary, who m. Sarah, only
dau. and heiress of Sir Thomas Cave, 6th Bt. and d. 13 Sept. 1815.

11. All black background

Two elliptical shields
Dexter shield   Otway   In pretence: (ensigned with a baroness'
coronet) Qly of thirty-five, 1st, Cave, 2nd, Sable on a bend between
three molets or three escallops gules (Bromflete), 3rd, Ermine on a bend
sable three wyverns' heads erased argent (Genill), 4th, Argent a chevron
between three popinjays vert membered gules (Cliffe), 5th, Gules a
chevron between three molets of six points or (Danvers), 6th, Argent on
a bend gules three martlets or winged vert (Danvers), 7th, Argent on a
bend gules three chevronels or (Brulie), 8th, Argent on a fess between
three martlets sable three molets argent (Pury), 9th, Sable on a fess
argent between three anchors or three lions' heads erased gules langued
azure (Wenman), 10th, Per pale purpure and azure over all a cross
argent (Wenman), 11th, Azure two chevrons or, on a canton argent a
Paschal Lamb couchant gules (   ), 12th, Argent a fess vert over all a
lion rampant gules (Whittingham), 13th, Argent a saltire engrailed
sable, on a chief sable two molets pierced argent (Iwardby), 14th, Or
on a cross engrailed gules another plain sable, in dexter chief a Cornish
chough proper (Mussenden), 15th, Argent two bars and in chief a
lion passant guardant sable (Frome), 16th, Or fretty gules, on a chief
or a lion passant guardant gules (   ), 17th, Azure a lion rampant
between seven cross crosslets or, on the lion's shoulder a fleur-de-lys
gules (   ), 18th, Azure three bars vairy ermine and gules (   ), 19th,
Gules two bendlets, one or, the other argent (Milo, Earl of Hereford),
20th, Gules three lozenges conjoined in fess or (Newmarch), 21st, Or
two lions passant guardant in pale gules (   ), 22nd, Vair three bendlets
gules (Braye), 23rd, Argent a chevron between three eagles' legs erased
sable (Braye), 24th, Or on a bend gules three goats passant argent attired
or (   ), 25th, Sable a chevron between three bulls' heads cabossed
argent (Norbury), 26th, Argent a fess between six cross crosslets azure
(Boteler), 27th, Gules two bars argent (Pantulphe), 28th, Or fretty

gules (Verdon), 29th, Argent two bends azure (   ), 30th, Or two
bendlets gules (Sudeley), 31st, Or four bendlets azure (Montford), 32nd,
Sable a lion rampant between eight billets argent (De La Planche), 33rd,
as 26th, 34th, Sable a cross between four bees erect or (Croysier), 35th,
Azure a chevron or (Dabernon)
Sinister shield (ensigned with a baroness's coronet), Qly of thirty-five as
on dexter shield, except 18th, argent not azure, and 31st, three bendlets
not four
Supporters: Two lions guardant or wings endorsed vair
For Sarah, only dau. and heiress of Sir Thomas Cave, 6th Bt., who m.
Henry Otway, of Castle Otway, co. Tipperary, and became Baroness
Braye on the termination of the abeyance of the barony in 1839.
She d. 21 Feb. 1862.
(There is a duplicate of this hatchment in the parish church of Swinford,
Leics)

12. Sinister background black

Gules on a chevron engrailed argent two lions passant counter passant
gules in chief two crosses formy argent (Richardson)   In pretence:
Qly of six, 1st, qly i & iv, Azure fretty argent (Cave) ii & iii, Argent a
pile sable a chevron counterchanged (Otway), 2nd, Cave, 3rd, Azure on
a cross argent five molets gules (Verney), 4th, Vair three bendlets gules
(Braye), 5th, Argent a chevron between three eagles' legs erased sable
armed gules (Braye), 6th, Or on a bend gules three goats passant argent
(Hallighwell)
For Anne, dau. of Henry Otway and Sarah, Baroness Braye. She m. 1st,
J.A. Arnold of Lutterworth, and 2nd, 1847, the Rev. Henry Kemp
Richardson, Rector of Leire, Leics, and d. 22 May 1871.

13. All black background

On a lozenge   Qly, 1st, Gules a chevron engrailed or ermined sable
between three lions' heads erased ermine ducally crowned or (Pyndar,
afterwards Lygon), 2nd, Argent two lions passant in pale tails fourché
gules (Lygon), 3rd, Gules three lions passant argent (?Gifford), 4th,
Gules a fess between six martlets or (Beauchamp of Powyke)
In pretence: Qly of six, 1st, qly i & iv, Azure fretty argent (Cave), ii
& iii, Argent a pile sable a chevron counterchanged (Otway), 2nd, Cave,
3rd, Azure on a cross argent five molets gules (Verney), 4th, Vair three
bendlets gules (Braye), 5th, Argent a chevron between three eagles'
legs erased sable armed gules (Braye), 6th, Or on a bend gules three
goats passant argent (Hallighwell)
Countess's coronet   Supporters: Dexter, A bear proper muzzled,
collared and chained or   Sinister, A swan argent wings endorsed
gules, beaked and legged sable, gorged with a ducal coronet and lined
or   On the breast of each supporter, suspended from the collar and
coronet, an escutcheon, Gules a fess between six martlets or
For Catherine, 4th dau. of Baroness Braye, who m. 1st, Henry, son of

Lord George Murray, and 2nd, John Reginald, 3rd Earl Beauchamp, and
d. 4 Nov. 1875.
(There is a duplicate of this hatchment in the parish church at
Swinford, Leics)

14. All black background
On a lozenge
Qly of six, 1st, qly Cave & Otway, 2nd, Cave, 3rd, Verney, 4th, Braye,
5th, Braye, 6th, Hallighwell (as E. of P. of 12.)
Probably for the Hon. Maria Otway Cave, eldest dau. of Sarah, Baroness
Braye. She d. unm. 13 May 1879.

15. All black background
Qly, 1st and 4th, qly i & iv, Argent on a chevron sable between three
cinquefoils gules three bezants (Edgell), ii & iii, Sable a fess dancetty
argent between three eagles displayed or, a chief or (Wyatt), 2nd and
3rd, qly of six, i. qly Cave & Otway, ii, Cave, iii, Verney, iv, Braye, v,
Braye, vi, Hallighwell; in centre chief a label argent
Crests: Dexter, A demi-lion rampant proper holding in its dexter paw a
cinquefoil gules slipped and leaved vert (Edgell)   Sinister, A demi-lion
rampant per pale crenelly or and sable holding in its dexter paw an
arrow gules feathered and headed or (Wyatt)
Mantling: Sable and argent   Motto: Honesta bona
In base skull and crossbones and words in scroll 'Or Glory'
For Edmund Verney, son of the Rev. Edgell Wyatt-Edgell, who d. 4
July 1879.

16. Sinister background black
Two lozenges   Dexter lozenge, Qly, 1st and 4th, Edgell, 2nd and 3rd,
Wyatt   In pretence: Qly, 1st, Cave, 2nd, Verney, 3rd, Braye, 4th,
Braye, the escutcheon ensigned with a baroness's coronet
Sinister lozenge, Qly as escutcheon of pretence of dexter lozenge, and
ensigned with a baroness's coronet
Supporters: Two lions guardant or wings endorsed vair
For Henrietta, Baroness Braye, youngest dau. of Henry Otway and
Sarah, Baroness Braye.   She m. the Rev. Edgell Wyatt-Edgell,
became Baroness Braye on the death of her sister Maria, and d. 14
Nov. 1879.

17. All black background
Qly, 1st and 4th, Wyatt, 2nd and 3rd, Edgell   In pretence: Qly, 1st
and 4th, qly i & iv Cave, ii & iii Otway, 2nd and 3rd, Argent a chevron
between three eagles' legs erased sable armed gules (Braye), the
escutcheon ensigned with a baron's coronet
Crests: Wyatt and Edgell, as 15.
Mantling: Sable and argent   Motto: Honesta bona
For the Rev. Edgell Wyatt-Edgell, who m. the Hon. Henrietta Otway

Cave, youngest dau. of Baroness Braye, and d. 26 Sept. 1888.
(B.P. 1896 ed.)
(There is a duplicate of this hatchment in the parish church of Swinford,
Leics)

STOKE BRUERN

1. All black background
On a lozenge surmounted by a cherub's head
Sable six swallows, three, two and one argent (Arundel)
Skull below
Probably for Elizabeth, dau. of Francis Arundel, of Stoke Park. She d.
15 Feb. 1730/1.

THENFORD

1. All black background
Argent on a chevron sable nine bezants (Severne)   In pretence: Qly,
1st and 4th, Paly embattled of eight argent and gules (Wigley), 2nd and
3rd, Argent a fess between three cinquefoils pierced sable (Meysey)
Crest: A cinquefoil or   Mantling: Or and argent
Motto: Virtus praestantior auro
For John Michael Severne, who m. Anna Maria, dau. of Edmund Meysey
Wigley, of Shakenhurst, co. Worcester, and d. 15 Aug. 1855.
(B.L.G. 7th ed.)

THORP MALSOR HALL

1. Dexter background black
Qly, 1st and 4th, Argent a chevron between three maunches sable
(Maunsell), 2nd, Argent three cocks gules (Cockayne), 3rd, Gules
three lions passant guardant per pale or and argent (O'Brien), impaling
to dexter, Sable a chevron argent between three crescents or (Palmer),
impaling to sinister, Argent a fret sable (Tollemache)
Crest: A hawk rising proper, with motto, 'Quod vult valde vult'
Mantling: Sable and argent
Motto: Honorantes me honorabo
For the Rev. George Edmond Maunsell, who m. 1st, 1846, Theodosia
Mary, dau. of Sir Henry Palmer, Bt. of East Carlton, and 2nd, 1869,
Matilda Anne Frances, dau. of the Rev. H.F. Tollemache, Rector of
Harrington, and d. 29 Oct. 1875.   (B.L.G. 7th ed.)

TWYWELL

1. Sinister background black
Azure on a chevron between three annulets or a lion passant azure
(Gunnell), impaling, Sable a bend engrailed between six billets argent
(Alington)
For Frances, dau. of the Rev. William Alington, Rector of Twywell,
who m. R. Pickering Gunnell of Woodford, and d. 5 Feb. 1866.
(B.L.G. 7th ed)

UFFORD

1. All black background
Or two bars azure a chief qly, 1st and 4th, Azure two fleurs-de-lys or,
2nd and 3rd, Gules a lion passant guardant or: in centre chief a molet
argent for cadency (Manners)
Peer's helm   Crest: On a chapeau gules and ermine a peacock in her
pride proper   Mantle: Gules and ermine   Motto: Pour y parvenir
Supporters: Two unicorns argent, armed, maned, unguled and tufted
or
Winged skull in base
Unidentified, see 2.

2. Exactly as 1. except that the cadency molet is sable and the helm is an esquire's, not a peer's.
Possibly both 1. and 2. are intended for James Manners, youngest son
of John, 2nd Duke of Rutland.   He d. 1 Nov. 1790.   (B.P. 1949
ed.)

UPTON

1. Dexter background black
Argent two squirrels sejant addorsed cracking nuts gules (Samwell),
impaling, Sable a cross of fusils argent over all a bend ermine
(Godschalk)
Crest: On a ducal coronet or a squirrel sejant cracking a nut proper
No mantling   Motto: In coelo quies
For Sir Thomas Samwell, 1st Bt., who m. 1st, Elizabeth, dau. and
heiress of George Gooday of Bower Hall, Essex, and 2nd, Ann, dau. and
heiress of John Godschalk, of Atherston, co. Warwick. He was created
a baronet in 1675, and d. 3 March 1693/4. (Baker i. 224)
(N.B. This hatchment does not appear to be as old as 1694, and is
probably a replacement)

2. Dexter background black

Ermine two squirrels sejant addorsed cracking nuts gules, in centre chief
the Badge of Ulster (Samwell), impaling, Azure three escallops or
between two flaunches ermine (Clarke)
Crest: On a ducal coronet or a squirrel sejant proper
Mantling: Gules and argent, ending in tasselled cords   No motto
Unusual gilt decorative border to arms
For Sir Thomas Samwell, 2nd Bt., who m. 1st, 1710, Millicent, dau. and
heiress of the Rev. Thomas Fuller, and 2nd, 1721, Mary, dau. of Sir
Gilbert Clarke, and d. 16 Nov. 1757.

3. All black background

Argent two squirrels sejant addorsed gules (Samwell)
Crest: On a ducal coronet or a squirrel sejant gules
No mantling   Motto: Christus sit regula vitae
For Sir Thomas Samwell, 3rd Bt., who d. unm. 3 Dec. 1779.

4. Sinister background black

Ermine two squirrels sejant addorsed cracking nuts gules, in sinister
chief the Badge of Ulster (Samwell), impaling, Azure two bars wavy
ermine, on a chief argent a demi-lion rampant sable (Smith)
Crest: Within a ducal coronet or a squirrel gules   Motto: Resurgam
Cherub's head at each angle of shield, which is flanked by leafy
branches
Skull in base
For Elizabeth, dau. of Thomas Smith of East Haddon, who m. Sir
Wenman Samwell, 4th Bt., and d. 28 June 1789.

WADENHOE

1. All black background

Per pale argent and sable a saltire counterchanged, in chief a crescent
argent for cadency (Hunt), impaling, Argent a leopard's face or
between two flaunches sable (Parker)
Crest: A talbot sejant argent   No helm or mantling
Motto: Mors janua vitae
Possibly for George Eden Hunt, who m. Margaret, dau. of Sir
William Parker, 9th Bt., and d. 28 Feb. 1892.   (B.L.G. 7th ed.)

WELTON PLACE

1. Dexter background black

Argent on a bend gules between three roundels sable three swans rising
argent (Clarke)   In pretence: Gules a chevron ermine between three

eagles close argent (Child)
Crest: A swan rising argent gorged with a coronet and chained or
Mantling: Gules and ermine   Motto: In Christ is my hope
For John Plomer Clarke, who m. Mary, dau. and heiress of Nicholas
Child of London, and d. 9 Jan. 1805.   (Baker i. 460)

2. All black background
On a lozenge   Clarke with Child in pretence
Mantling: Gules and argent
For Mary, widow of John Plomer Clarke,   She d. 25 Dec. 1816.

3. Dexter background black
Qly, 1st and 4th, Clarke, 2nd and 3rd, Child, impaling, Argent on a
pale sable a sword erect argent pomel and hilt or (Nelthorpe)
Crest, mantling and motto: As 1.
For John Plomer Clarke, who m. 1806, Anna Maria Charlotte, dau. of
Sir John Nelthorpe, Bt., of Scawby, Lincs, and d. 23 March 1826.

WHISTON

1. Dexter background black
Argent fretty sable on a canton gules a chaplet or, in centre chief the
Badge of Ulster (Irby), impaling, Argent three wolves' heads erased
proper (Methuen)
Baron's coronet   Crest: A Saracen's head in profile proper, wreathed
at the temples or   Motto: Honor fidelitatis praemium
Supporters: Two antelopes gules each gorged with a chaplet or
For Frederick, 2nd Baron Boston, who m. 1775, Christiana, only dau.
of Paul Methuen, Corsham House, Wilts, and d. 23 March 1825.
(B.P. 1928 ed.)

2. All black background
On a lozenge   Irby, with Badge of Ulster, impaling, Methuen
Baroness' coronet
Supporters: As 1.
For Christiana, widow of Frederick, 2nd Baron Boston.   She d. 9 May
1832.

3. Sinister background black
Irby   In pretence: Argent a wyvern wings displayed and tail nowed
gules (Drake)
Baron's coronet   Supporters: As 1.
For Rachel, dau. and co-heiress of William Drake, of Amersham, Bucks,
who m. 1801, George, 3rd Baron Boston, and d. 6 April 1830.

WOLLASTON

1. All black background
Qly, 1st and 4th, Ermine a cross patonce sable charged with a leopard's face or (Dickins), 2nd and 3rd, Or a cross engrailed per pale gules and sable, on a chief sable a lion passant guardant or (Brooke)
Crest: A lion couchant or holding in its dexter gamb a cross patonce sable
Mantling: Gules and or
Probably for Ambrose Dickins, who d. 2 Sept. 1793.

YARDLEY HASTINGS

1. All black background
Sable a lion passant guardant or between three esquires' helmets argent (Compton)
Earl's coronet   Crest: On a mount a beacon fired proper and a ribbon inscribed with the words 'Nisi Dominus'
Mantling: Gules and argent   Motto: Je ne cherche que ung
Supporters: Two dragons ermine ducally gorged and chained or
Possibly for Charles John Spencer, Earl Compton, d. unm. 5 Sept. 1887.   (B.P. 1928 ed.)

2. All black background
Argent on a chevron engrailed azure between three rooks proper three suns or (Rooke)
Crest: A rook feeding on a wheatsheaf or
Mantling: Azure and argent   Motto: Nos pascit deus
For the Rev. George Rooke, Rector of Yardley Hastings, who d. unm. 24 Sept. 1856.   (Tablet in church)

LOWER HEYFORD HOUSE

1. Dexter background black
Qly, 1st and 4th, Argent a fess between six cross crosslets fitchy gules (Craven), 2nd and 3rd, Or five fleurs-de-lys in cross sable a chief wavy azure (Craven ancient), impaling to dexter, Azure an eagle displayed argent, on a chief embattled argent three roundels azure (Raymond), and impaling to sinister, Argent a lion rampant gules (Hughes)
Crest: On a chapeau gules and ermine a griffin statant argent
Mantling: Gules and argent   Motto: Mors janua vitae
Shield flanked by palm branches
For the Rev. John Craven, of Chilton House, Wilts, who m. 1st, Elizabeth, dau. of Sir Jermett Raymond, and 2nd, Catherine, dau. of James Hughes of Litcomb, Berks, and d. 19 June 1804.

WARWICKSHIRE

Grendon: For Walter Chetwynd, 1692
Photo: Chris J. Smith

INTRODUCTION

Within the boundaries of Warwickshire there are approximately one hundred and fifty-five hatchments and, if this total is not large in comparison with those of some other countries, it does include many interesting and varied examples.

The smallest and possibly the oldest is in Mancetter church and is less than two feet square. At the other end of the scale is the huge hatchment of Henry Greswolde Lewis in Yardley church, Birmingham; this must surely be one of the largest in Great Britain, measuring over seven feet square and enclosed within a heavily moulded frame.

Whilst many Warwickshire hatchments are maintained in excellent condition it is regrettable that some churches take no steps whatever to preserve these relics of the past. I know of several cases in which hatchments are rapidly deteriorating for want of a little attention and others could well benefit from careful wiping down to remove accumulations of dust and grime. I can recall one instance in recent years where two repairable hatchments were thrown out of a church in the county and have since been wantonly destroyed.

Several churches possess good collections for members of their patron families. For example, at Compton Wynyates there are twelve fine hatchments for Marquesses and Earls of Northampton and their wives, whilst Stoneleigh has nine for members of the Leigh family. Grendon possesses a similar number for the Chetwynds.

But one of the most interesting and controversial collections is in Solihull church. In addition to four conventional hatchments there are several small rectangular frames enclosing achievements or monograms on paper or canvas. The frames bear inscriptions stating that they served at the

45

funerals of specified persons and consequently there is some justification for regarding them as hatchments. Nevertheless, since there is some doubt as to their true purpose they have been omitted from this record.

In 1713 Sir Christopher Wren took up residence at Wroxall Abbey between Warwick and Birmingham and his hatchment hangs upon the wall of Wroxall church. It is a very good example from the early eighteenth century.

The only ecclesiastical specimen may be seen in the Cathedral of St. Chad in Birmingham. It is for a former Roman Catholic bishop of that city and is probably the most recent hatchment in the county.

Variety of design is a most noticeable feature of Warwickshire hatchments. Whilst in certain counties there is clear similarity of design, indicating perhaps the existence of firms of hatchment specialists using set patterns, there is little or no evidence of such practice in Warwickshire.

Armorial boards, of which there are about a dozen in the county's churches, have not been included in this work as they are unlikely to have had any funerary significance.

G.A. Harrison
6 Mardu, near Clun, Salop.

ANSLEY

1. Dexter background black
Barry of ten argent and azure a lion rampant gules (Stratford),
impaling, Vert three horses courant argent (   )
Crest: An arm in armour proper garnished or, in the hand a scimitar
argent hilted or   Mantling: Gules and argent
Unidentified

2. Dexter background black
Qly, 1st, Azure a chevron between three boars' heads couped or
(Ludford), 2nd, Gules three lions' gambs erased argent (Newdigate),
3rd, Vairy argent and sable a fess gules (Bracebridge), 4th, Azure on a
chevron between three boars' heads couped or three fleurs -de lys gules
(Ludford), impaling, Argent five fusils conjoined in fess gules in chief
three bears' heads sable muzzled argent (Boswell)
Crests: Dexter, A boar's head couped or (Ludford) Sinister, A fleur -
de -lys argent (Newdigate)
Mantling: Gules and argent   Motto: Confide recte agens
Winged skull in base
For John Newdigate Ludford, who m. Elizabeth, dau. of John Boswell,
and d. 1822.

3. All black background
On an ornate curved lozenge
Arms: As 2.
Motto: Christus spes mea
Cherub's head above, winged skull below and greenish cloth behind
lozenge
For Elizabeth, dau. of John Boswell, and widow of John Newdigate
Ludford.   She d.

4. Sinister background black
Qly argent and gules four crosses formy counterchanged, in dexter chief
the Badge of Ulster (Chetwode)   In pretence: Ludford qly, as 2.
Mantle: Gules and argent, cords and tassels or
Winged cherub's head above
For Elizabeth Juliana, dau. and heir of John Newdigate Ludford, who
m. Sir John Newdigate-Ludford-Chetwode, 5th Bt. and d. 1859.
(B.P. 1938 ed.)

5. All black background
Arms: As 4.
Crests: Dexter, Out of a ducal coronet or a demi-lion rampant gules
(Chetwode)   Sinister, A boar's head couped or (Ludford)
Mantling: Gules and argent   Motto: Resurgam
Winged skull below
For Sir John Newdigate-Ludford-Chetwode, 5th Bt., d. 1873.

6. Dexter background black
Qly, 1st and 4th, Azure a chevron between three boars' heads couped
or (Ludford), 2nd and 3rd, Vairy argent and sable a fess gules
(Bracebridge)
Crest: A boar's head couped or   No mantling or motto
Cherub's head below
For John Bracebridge Ludford, who m. Juliana, dau. and heir of Sir
Richard Newdigate, 3rd Bt. and d. 1775.

7. All black background
On an elaborate curvilinear lozenge flanked by palm branches
Arms: As 6.
For Juliana, widow of John Bracebridge Ludford. She d. 1780.

ARROW

1. Dexter background black
Two oval shields   Dexter, surrounded by the Garter, Qly, 1st and 4th,
Sable on a bend cotised argent a rose gules between two annulets sable
(Conway), 2nd, qly i and iv, Or on a pile gules between six fleurs-de-lys
azure three lions passant guardant or (Seymour Augmentation), ii &
iii, Gules two wings conjoined in lure or (Seymour), 3rd, Ermine on a
fess gules three escallops or a canton gules (Ingram)   Sinister, Qly, as
dexter shield   In pretence: Qly, 1st and 4th, Ermine on a fess gules
three escallops or (Ingram), 2nd, Azure a chevron between three
lions passant or (   ), 3rd, Sable three greyhounds courant argent
within a bordure argent (   )
Marquess' coronet   Crest: A moor's head in profile couped at the
shoulders proper wreathed at the temples argent and azure
Mantle: Gules and ermine   Motto: Fide et amore
Supporters: Two moors proper habited on the body and legs or, from
the waist a skirt gules with feathers pendent vert, like feathers from
the shoulders terminating in lions' faces; wreathed about the temples
argent and sable, holding in the exterior hands shields azure, on the
dexter a sun in splendour and on the sinister a crescent or
For Francis, 2nd Marquess of Hertford, who m. 2nd, Isabella Anne
Ingram-Shepherd, dau. and co-heir of Charles Ingram, 9th Viscount
Irvine, and d. 1822. (B.P. 1938 ed.)

2. Dexter background black
Two oval shields   Dexter, surrounded by the Garter, Qly, 1st and 4th,
Conway, 2nd and 3rd, qly i and iv, Seymour Augmentation, ii & iii,
Seymour   Sinister, Qly, as dexter shield, impaling, Argent a double-
headed eagle displayed sable (?Fagnani)
Pendent below the dexter shield are the Collar of the Order of the
Garter and the badges of two other Orders   Marquess' coronet
Crests: Dexter, A moor's head in profile couped at the shoulders proper

wreathed at the temples argent and azure　　Sinister, From a ducal
coronet or a phoenix issuant proper wings elevated argent　　Mantle:
Gules and ermine　　Motto: Fide et amore　　Supporters: As 1.
For Francis Charles, 3rd Marquess of Hertford, who m. Maria Fagnani,
illegitimate dau. of William, 4th Duke of Queensberry by Marquesa
Constanza Fagnani, and d. 1842. (B.P. 1938 ed.)
(There are duplicates of these two hatchments in the parish church of
Sudbourne, Suffolk)

BADDESLEY CLINTON

1. Dexter background black

Gules seven mascles conjoined three, three and one or (Ferrers),
impaling, Argent a cross flory between four martlets gules a canton
azure (Bird)
Crest: A unicorn passant ermine, crined, armed and unguled or
Mantling: Gules and argent　　Motto: Mors janua vitae
Skull and cross-bones in base
For Edward Ferrers who m. Hester, dau. of Christopher Bird of London,
and d. 1794. (B.L.G. 1871 ed.)

2. Dexter background black

Qly, 1st, Gules seven mascles conjoined three, three and one or
(Ferrers), 2nd, Sable six horseshoes argent (Ferrers), 3rd, Vairy or and
gules (Ferrers), 4th, Or a cross patonce gules (Freville), impaling, Qly, 1st
Azure a chevron ermine between three escallops argent (Townshend), 2nd,
England quartering France within a bordure argent (　　), 3rd, Sable a
lion passant or between three esquires' helmets argent (Compton), 4th,
Paly of six or and azure a canton ermine (Shirley), 5th, Argent a cross
engrailed gules between four water bougets sable (Bourchier), 6th, Vairy
or and gules (Ferrers)
Crest: A unicorn passant proper　　Mantling: Gules and argent
Motto: Splendeo tritus
For Edward Ferrers, who m. Harriet Anne Ferrers, 2nd dau. and co-heir
of George, 2nd Marquess Townshend, and d. 1830.

BARSTON

1. All black background

Or a kingfisher proper (Fisher), impaling, Gules on a fess argent between
three boars' heads couped or a lion passant azure (Gough)
Crest: A kingfisher holding in the beak a fish proper
Mantling: Gules and argent　　Motto: Post funera virtus
For John Fisher of Springfield, who m. Margaret, dau. of Walter Gough of
Perry Hall, and d. 1754. (monument in church and B.L.G. 1848 ed.)

2. **Sinister background black**
Or a lion rampant queue-fourché gules (   ), impaling, Or a kingfisher
proper (Fisher)
Crest: ?A falcon proper   Mantling: Gules and argent
Motto: Non est mortale quod opto
Unidentified

BERKSWELL

1. All black background
On a lozenge   Qly, 1st, Qly ermine and paly of six or and gules
(Knightley), 2nd, Ermine a rose gules barbed and seeded proper
(   ), 3rd, Azure a fess engrailed or between three maidens' busts
couped at the shoulders proper crined or (Marow), 4th, Azure on a
chevron argent between three pheons points downwards or three
crosses formy gules (Wightwick), impaling, Azure six annulets, three,
two and one or (Musgrave)
Motto: Mors janua vitae   Skull and cross-bones in top angle
For Catherine Musgrave, who m. John Knightly, alias Wightwick, and
d. 1812.

2. Sinister background black
Qly, 1st, Sable on a fess or between three eagles' heads couped argent
three escallops gules (Wilmot), 2nd, Argent on a chevron azure three
garbs or, on a canton gules a fret or (Eardley), 3rd, Azure a fess
engrailed or between three maidens' busts couped at the shoulders
proper crined or (Marow), 4th, Qly argent and sable on a bend gules
three molets argent (Cayley), impaling, Qly, 1st and 4th, Argent a
fess between three lozenges sable (Parry), 2nd, Argent a lion rampant
azure (   ), 3rd, Argent a cross crosslet fitchy sable between three
fleurs-de-lys gules (Hillier)
Mantling: Gules and argent   Shield flanked by two cherubs' heads
and two more above
For Elizabeth, dau. of Dr Caleb Hillier Parry, who m. Sir John
Eardley Eardley-Wilmot, 1st Bt. and d. 1818.   (B.P. 1938 ed.)

3. Dexter background black
Qly, as dexter of 2., impaling, Ermine on a chief sable a griffin passant
argent (Chester), at fess point of shield the Badge of Ulster
Crests: Dexter, An eagle's head argent in the beak an escallop gules
(Wilmot)   Sinister, A stag courant gules attired and unguled or
Mantle: Gules and argent
For Sir John Eardley Eardley-Wilmot, 1st Bt., who m. 2nd, 1819,
Elizabeth, dau. of Sir Robert Chester, of Bush Hall, co. Hertford, and
d. 3 Feb. 1847.

4. Dexter background black

Qly, 1st, Wilmot, (eagles' heads erased), 2nd, Argent a fess gules between three children's heads couped at the shoulders proper crined and habited or (Marow), 3rd, Qly azure and sable on a bend argent three molets gules (Cayley), 4th, Eardley, impaling, Qly 1st and 4th, Argent a tree eradicated proper ( ), 2nd and 3rd, Argent a chevron sable ermined argent ( )
Crest: An eagle's head erased argent in the beak an escallop gules
Mantle: Gules and argent   Motto: In coelo quies
Unidentified

5. All black background

Wilmot, as 4., impaling, Argent three bars and in chief three trivets sable (Rivett)
Crest: An eagle's head erased argent in the beak an escallop gules
Mantling: Gules and argent   Motto: Resurgam
For the Rt. Hon. Sir John Eardley Wilmot, Lord Chief Justice of the Court of Common Pleas, who m. Sarah, dau. of T. Rivett, M.P. and d. 1792.

BILTON

1. Sinister background black

Qly, 1st and 4th, Vert a lion rampant argent (Hume), 2nd and 3rd, Argent three popinjays vert beaked and legged gules (Pepdie)   In pretence: Sable three crescents or (Boughton)
Motto: Resurgam   Lover's knot and two cherubs' heads above shield which is flanked by palm branches
For Anna, sister and heir of Edward Boughton of Rugby, who m. as his 1st wife, Alexander Hume, Lord of the manor of Rugby, and d. 1777.

2. All black background

Qly, 1st and 4th, Per bend or ermined sable and sable a lion rampant per bend sable and or (for Simpson), 2nd and 3rd, Sable ten roundels argent, on a chief argent a lion passant guardant sable (for Bridgeman), impaling, Qly, 1st and 4th, Chequy ermine and sable (for Estwicke), 2nd and 3rd, Per pale argent and gules (Waldegrave)
No helm, crest, mantling or motto
For Grace, dau. of Samuel Estwicke, who m. the Hon. John Bridgeman Simpson, son of Henry, 1st Baron Bradford, and d. 1839.

BIRMINGHAM (St Chad's R.C. Cathedral)

1. Sinister background black
Argent on a chevron azure between three crosses potent gules three
broom cods slipped and leaved or (See of Birmingham), impaling,
Sable on a sevenfold mound a patriarchal cross, over all the word Pax
in fess or (?Ullathorne)
Shield surmounts a bishop's pastoral staff, is ensigned by a mitre,
and is surrounded by four gold fleurs-de-lys
For the Rt. Rev. William Bernard Ullathorne, O.S.B., Archbishop of
Birmingham, who d. 1888.

BIRMINGHAM

See also under, HALL GREEN, HANDSWORTH, KINGS NORTON
and YARDLEY

BOURTON-on-DUNSMORE

1. All black background
On an ornate curvilinear lozenge   Argent a chevron between three
molets sable (Shuckburgh), impaling, Or on a fess sable four escallops argent
(Venour)
Mantle: Gules and ermine, tasselled and corded or
For Sophia Venour, who m. John Shuckburgh, and d.18 Jan. 1848.
(mural monument in church)

2. All black background
Shuckburgh impaling Venour, as 1.
Crest: A blackamoor couped at the waist proper, habited argent, skirt
or, wreathed at the temples or and holding in the dexter hand an arrow
or   Mantling: Gules and argent   Motto: Vigilate et orate
For John Shuckburgh, who m. Sophia Venour, and d. 12 May 1837.
(mural monument in church)

3. Dexter background black
Qly, 1st and 4th, Sable a chevron between three molets argent
(Shuckburgh), 2nd and 3rd, Paly of six gules and ermine (Jermyn)
In pretence: Sable three swans wings expanded argent beaked and legged
gules (   )
Crest: A blackamoor couped at the waist proper, wearing a skirt paly
gules and argent, wreathed at the temples argent and gules, holding in
the dexter hand an arrow or feathered argent
Mantling: Gules and argent   Motto: Vigilate et orate
Skull and crossbones in base

For Colonel Richard Shuckburgh, who m. Catherine,
and d. 14 May 1762. (Ledger stone in church)

4. All black background
Sable a chevron indented or between three molets pierced argent, all
within a bordure or (Shuckburgh)
Crest: A demi-Moor proper wreathed at the temples or and sable,
habited argent, semy of molets pierced sable, holding in the dexter hand
an arrow point downwards argent
Mantle: Azure and or   Motto: Vigilate et orate
For the Rev. Charles Blencowe Shuckburgh, who d. s.p. 1875.

BUTLERS MARSTON

1. All black background
Azure a pale between two eagles displayed argent (Woodward)
Crest: Out of a ducal coronet or a greyhound sejant argent
Mantling: Gules and argent   Motto: Sub cruce triumpho
For Thomas Woodward, who d.

CHARLECOTE

1. Dexter background black
Gules three lucies hauriant between nine cross crosslets argent (Lucy),
impaling, Per fess or and azure a chevron gules between three molets
counterchanged, a canton of England (Lane)
Crest: Out of a ducal coronet gules a boar's head ermine bristled or
between two wings or billety sable
Mantle: Gules and ermine   Motto: Non nobis nascitur
For the Rev. John Hammond Lucy, who m. Maria, dau. of John Lane,
of Bentley Hall, Staffordshire, and d. 1823. (B.L.G. 1871 ed.)

2. All black background
Gules three lucies hauriant argent between nine cross crosslets or (Lucy)
Crest: Out of a ducal coronet gules a boar's head ermine between two
wings or billety sable
Mantle: Gules and argent   Motto: Post funera virtus   Skull in base
For George Lucy, d. unm. 1786.

3. All black background
Gules three lucies hauriant between nine cross crosslets argent (Lucy)
Crest: Out of a ducal coronet gules a boar's head ermine between two
wings sable billety or
Mantling: Gules and argent   Motto: By truth and diligence
For Thomas Lucy, who d. unm. 1744.

COMPTON WYNYATES

1. All black background
Qly, 1st and 4th, Sable a lion passant guardant or between three esquires helmets argent (Compton), 2nd and 3rd, Argent a chevron vert a bordure azure bezanty (Vannell)   In pretence: Qly, 1st Paly of six or and azure a canton ermine (Shirley), 2nd, Vairy or and gules (Ferrers), 3rd, Gules seven mascles conjoined, three, three and one or (Ferrers), 4th, Qly France and England a bordure argent (Thomas of Woodstock)
Earl's coronet.   Crest: On a mount vert a beacon fired proper, before it a riband inscribed NISI DOMINUS   Mantling: Gules and ermine
Motto: Je ne serche que ung
Supporters: Two dragons ermine ducally gorged and chained or
For James, 5th Earl of Northampton, who m. Elizabeth, Baroness Ferrers of Chartley, and d. 3 Oct. 1754.

2. Sinister background black
Arms, coronet, supporters and motto, as 1.
For Elizabeth, Baroness Ferrers, wife of James, 5th Earl of Northampton. She d. 1740.

3. Dexter background black
Sable a lion passant guardant or between three esquires helmets argent (Compton), impaling, Sable a fess between three leopards faces or (Payne)
Earl's coronet   Crest: On a mound vert a beacon fired proper, before it a riband inscribed NISI DOMINUS   Mantling: Gules and ermine   Motto: Je ne serche que ung
Supporters: Two dragons ermine ducally gorged and chained or
For George, 6th Earl of Northampton, who m. Frances, daughter of the Rev. Thomas Payne, and d.s.p. 6 Dec. 1758.

4. All black background
Sable a lion passant guardant or between three esquires helmets argent (Compton), impaling, Qly, France and England, within a bordure compony argent and azure (Beaufort)
Earl's coronet   Crest: On a mount vert a beacon fired proper
Mantling: Gules and ermine
Motto: Je ne serche que ung
Supporters: Dexter, A dragon ermine ducally gorged and chained or
Sinister, A panther argent, semy of roundels, gules azure and vert, collared and chained or, flames issuing from the mouth and ears proper
For Charles, 7th Earl of Northampton, who m. Anne, dau. of Charles, 4th Duke of Beaufort, and d. 18 Oct. 1763.

5. Sinister background black
Arms, coronet, supporters and motto, as 4.
For Anne, wife of Charles, 7th Earl of Northampton. She d.

6. All black background
Sable a lion passant guardant or between three esquires helmets argent
(Compton)   In pretence: Argent on a fess between three cross
crosslets fitchy sable a cinquefoil argent (Lawton)
Earl's coronet   Crest: On a mount vert a beacon fired proper, before
it a riband inscribed NISI DOMINUS   Motto: Je ne serce que ung
Supporters: Two dragons ermine ducally gorged and chained or
Skull and crossbones in base
For Spencer, 8th Earl of Northampton, who m. 1st, 1758, Jane, dau.
of Henry Lawton, and 2nd, Miss Hougham, and d. 7th Apr. 1796.

7. Sinister background black
Arms, coronet, supporters and motto, as 6.
For Jane, 1st wife of Spencer, 8th Earl of Northampton. She d. 26
Nov. 1767.

8. Dexter background black
Qly, 1st and 4th, Sable a lion passant guardant or between three
esquires helmets argent (Compton), 2nd and 3rd, Argent a chevron vert
a bordure azure bezanty (Vannell)   In pretence: Argent a saltire
between three crescents and in base a dolphin sable (Smith)
Marquess' coronet   Three crests: Dexter, a demi-dragon erased gules
around the waist a ducal coronet or   Centre, On a mount vert a beacon
fired proper, before it a riband inscribed with the words NISI DOMINUS
Sinister, A dragon proper holding a garb or   Mantle: Gules and ermine
Motto: Je ne cherche que ung
Supporters: Two dragons ermine ducally gorged and chained or
For Charles, 1st Marquess of Northampton, who m. Maria, dau. of
Joshua Smith of Erle Stoke Park, Wilts, and d. 24 May 1828.

9. All black background
On a lozenge   Qly, 1st and 4th, Sable a lion passant guardant or
between three esquires helmets argent (Compton), 2nd and 3rd,
Argent a chevron vert within a bordure azure bezanty (Vannell)
In pretence: Argent a saltire azure between three crescents gules and in
base a millrind azure (Smith)
Mantle: Gules and ermine   Supporters: Two dragons ermine ducally
gorged and chained or
For Maria, widow of Charles, 1st Marquess of Northampton. She d.
24 Mar. 1843.

10. All black background
Qly, 1st and 4th, Sable a lion passant guardant or between three
esquires helmets argent (Compton), 2nd and 3rd, Argent a chevron
vert within a bordure azure bezanty (Vannell)   In pretence: Qly,
1st and 4th, Argent a lion rampant gules in the dexter chief a helmet
proper (Clephane), 2nd, qly, i, Argent a lion rampant gules (   ), ii,

Azure a castle argent (   ), iii Or an arm in armour from the sinister
fesswise proper holding a cross crosslet fitchy sable (Maclean), iv, Or a
lymphad sable (   ), 3rd, Argent a human heart gules crowned or,
within a bordure azure charged with molets argent (Douglas)
Crest: On a mount vert a beacon fired proper before it a riband
inscribed with the words NISI DOMINUS   Motto: Je ne cherche que
ung   Supporters: Two dragons ermine ducally gorged and chained or
For Spencer Joshua Alwyne, 2nd Marquess of Northampton, who m.
Margaret, dau. of Major-General Douglas Maclean Clephane, and d. 17
Jan. 1851.

11. Sinister background black
Qly, 1st and 4th, Sable a lion passant guardant or between three
esquires helmets argent (Compton), 2nd and 3rd, Argent a chevron
vert within a bordure azure bezanty (Vannell)   In pretence: Qly,
1st and 4th, Argent a lion rampant gules holding up an esquires helmet
proper (Clephane), 2nd, qly, i, Azure a lion rampant argent (   ), ii,
Azure a castle argent pennant flying gules (   ), iii, Argent a cubit
arm in armour fesswise to the sinister, holding in the hand proper a
cross crosslet fitchy azure (Maclean), iv. Argent a galley sable (   ),
3rd, Argent a human heart gules ensigned with a royal crown proper,
within a bordure azure charged alternately with buckles or and
molets argent (Douglas)
Supporters: Two dragons ermine ducally gorged and chained or
For Margaret, wife of Spencer Joshua Alwyne, 2nd Marquess of
Northampton. She d. 2 Apr. 1830.

12. Sinister background black
Qly, 1st and 4th, Sable a lion passant guardant or between three
esquires helmets argent (Compton), 2nd and 3rd, qly i & iv, Argent
a human heart gules imperially crowned or on a chief azure three
molets argent (Douglas), ii & iii, Argent three piles gules, the two
exterior each charged with a molet argent, within a bordure azure
charged with eight buckles or (Douglas), impaling, Azure a bend or,
on a chief or two choughs proper (Vyner)
Marchioness's coronet   Supporters: Dexter, A dragon ermine
Sinister, A unicorn argent crined and unguled sable
For Theodosia, dau. of Capt. and Lady Mary Vyner, who m.
Charles, 3rd Marquess of Northampton, and d.s.p. 18 Nov. 1864.

COUGHTON

1. Dexter background black
Qly, 1st and 4th, Gules on a chevron argent three bars gemel sable
(Throckmorton), 2nd and 3rd, Argent a fess between three gates sable
(Yate), over all the Badge of Ulster, impaling, Azure three stirrups

leathered or (Giffard)
Crest: An elephant's head erased sable, eared or tusked argent
Mantling: Gules and argent   Motto: Virtus sola nobilitas
For Sir John Courtenay Throckmorton, 5th Bt., who m. 1782, Maria
Catherine, dau. of Thomas Giffard of Chillington, and d. 3 Jan. 1819.
(B.P. 1889 ed.)   (There is a duplicate of this hatchment in the parish
church of Buckland, Berkshire)

2. Dexter background black
Gules on a chevron argent three bars gemel sable, in middle chief the
Badge of Ulster (Throckmorton), impaling, Argent a lion rampant
sable (Stapleton)
Crest: An elephant's head erased sable, eared or tusked argent
Motto: Mors Janua vitae
For Sir George Courtenay Throckmorton, 6th Bt., who m. 1792,
Catherine, only dau. of Thomas Stapleton of Carlton, Yorkshire, and
d. 16 July 1826.

3. All black background
Gules on a chevron argent five bars sable, in chief the Badge of Ulster
(for Throckmorton), impaling, Azure a fess dancetty the upper points
terminating in fleurs-de-lys or (Plowden)
Crest: An elephant's head couped proper
Motto: Virtus sola nobilitas
For Sir Charles Throckmorton, 7th Bt., who m. 1787, Mary, dau. of
Edmund Plowden of Plowden, Salop. and d. 3 Dec. 1840.

ELMDON

1. All black background
Azure a boar's head couped in bend or distilling drops of blood from
the neck proper (Spooner), impaling, Argent three pallets gules
within a bordure engrailed or, on a canton gules a spur leathered
or (Knight)
Crest: A boar's head couped or pierced through the neck with a spear
proper   Mantle: Gules and argent   Motto: In coelo quies
Cherub's head on either side of shield
For Abraham Spooner, who m. Anne, dau. of Richard Knight of
Downton Castle, Herefordshire, and d. 1788. (B.L.G. 1871 ed.)
(This hatchment was in poor condition when recorded in 1961 and
has since been destroyed)

2. Dexter background black
Azure ten estoiles, four, three, two and one or, on a chief argent
a crescent reversed gules between two boars' heads coupled sable
(Alston)
Crest: A demi-eagle wings expanded and inverted proper, on

each wing a crescent reversed gules.

Mantling: Gules and argent (no helm)   Motto: In altum

For William Charles Alston, d.

(This hatchment was in poor condition when recorded in 1961 and has since been destroyed)

ETTINGTON

1. Dexter background black

Qly, 1st and 4th, Paly of six or and azure a canton ermine (Shirley), 2nd and 3rd, qly i. and iv., France, ii and iii. England, all within a bordure argent (Plantagenet), impaling, Azure three molets pierced sable (Wollaston)

Crest: A Saracen's head in profile couped at the neck proper, wreathed at the temples or and azure

Mantling: Gules and argent   Motto: In coelo quies

Winged skull in base

For Evelyn Shirley, who m. 1781, Phillis Byan, only dau. of Charlton Wollaston, M.D., F.R.S., and d. 1 May 1810. (B.L.G. 1871 ed.)

2. Dexter background black

Qly, 1st and 4th, Paly of six or and azure a quarter ermine (Shirley), 2nd and 3rd, Argent a fess gules in chief three roundels gules (Devereux)

In pretence: Qly ermine and gules (Stanhope)

Crest: As 1.   Mantle: Gules and argent, tasselled or

Motto: Honor virtutis praemium   Badges: Dexter, A horseshoe or

Sinister, A Bourchier knot argent

For Evelyn John Shirley, who m. 1810, Eliza, only dau. and heir of Arthur Stanhope, and d. 31 Dec. 1856.

3. Al black background

On a lozenge

Paly of six or and azure a qurter ermine (Shirley), impaling, Qly ermine and gules (Stanhope)

For Eliza, widow of Evelyn John Shirley, She d. 30 Apr. 1859.

4. Dexter background black

Paly of six or and azure a quarter ermine (Shirley), impaling, Gules a fess in chief two pelicans vulning themselves or (Lechmere)

Crest and badges: As 2.(tinctures of badges reversed)

Mantle: Azure and argent   Motto: Loyal je suis

For Evelyn Philip Shirley, who m. 1842, Mary Clara Elizabeth, dau. of Sir Edmund Hungerford Lechmere, 2nd Bt. and d. 19 Sept. 1882.

FILLONGLEY

1. Sinister background black

Qly, 1st, Argent on a bend azure three mascles argent (Adderley), 2nd, Ermine a fess chequy or and azure (Arden), 3rd, Argent a lion rampant between three cross crosslets gules (Bowyer), 4th, Azure crusilly a lion rampant argent (Kynnersley), impaling, Ermine on a chief indented sable three escallops argent (Taylor)

Crest: On a chapeau gules and ermine a stork argent
Mantle: Gules and ermine corded and tasselled or
For Caroline, dau. of John Taylor of Moseley Hall, who m. George William Bowyer Adderley of Fillongley House, and d. 18..
(B.L.G. 1871 ed.)

GRENDON

1. Dexter background

Qly, 1st and 4th, Azure a chevron between three molets or (Chetwynd), 2nd and 3rd, Argent two chevrons gules (Grendon), in centre chief the Badge of Ulster   In pretence: Argent three roses gules barbed and seeded proper a chief gules (Sparrow)

Crest: A goat's head erased proper, armed and bearded or
Mantling: Gules and argent   Motto: Quod deus vult fiet
For Sir George Chetwynd, 2nd Bt., who m. Hannah Maria, dau. and co-heir of John Sparrow of Bishton Hall, Staffs, and d. 1850.
(B.P. 1938 ed.)

2. Dexter background black

Qly of six, 1st and 6th, Azure a chevron between three molets or (Chetwynd), 2nd, Argent two bars gules (   ), 3rd, Argent two chevrons gules (Grendon), 4th, Argent on a cross engrailed sable five molets or (Frodsham), 5th, Gules three roaches in pale argent (Delaroche)   In pretence, and impaling, Argent a chevron between three annulets gules (Goring)

Crest and mantling: As 1.   Motto: In coelo quies
For Walter Chetwynd, who m. Barbara, dau. and heir of John Goring of Kingston, Staffs, and d. 1713.

3. All black background

On a lozenge   Qly of six, with escutcheon of pretence and impalement as 2.
For Barbara, dau. of John Goring, and widow of Walter Chetwynd. She d. 1763.

4. All black background

Azure a chevron between three molets or (Chetwynd)

Crest: A goat's head erased argent armed or
Mantling: Gules and argent   Motto: Mors janua vitae
Possibly for James Chetwynd, who d. unm. 1774.

5. All black background

Qly, 1st and 4th, Sable a chevron between three molets or (Chetwynd),
2nd, Argent two chevrons gules (Grendon), 3rd, Qly, i & iv, Argent
three roses argent seeded proper, a chief gules (Sparrow), ii & iii,
Argent a chevron sable between three square buckles (brown)
(Moreton), impaling, Qly, 1st, Sable on a fess argent between three
leopards passant guardant or, spotted sable, three escallops gules (Hill),
2nd, Per bend sinister ermine and sable ermined argent a lion rampant
or (Tudor Trevor), 3rd, Or a lion rampant gules ducally gorged or
(   ), 4th, Qly, i & iv, Gules a quatrefoil vert (Rowe), ii & iii, Argent a
chevron sable between three trefoils vert (Rowe)   In centre chief of
shield the Badge of Ulster
Crest: A goat's head argent armed or
No mantling   Motto: Quod deus vult fiet
For Sir George Chetwynd, 3rd Bt. who m. 1843, Charlotte Augusta,
dau. of Arthur, 3rd Marquess of Downshire, and d. 24 Mar. 1869.

6. Dexter background black

Qly, 1st and 4th, Azure a chevron between three molets or (Chetwynd),
2nd and 3rd, Argent two chevrons gules (Grendon), at fess point on
dexter the Badge of Ulster, impaling, Argent two bars sable (Bantin)
Crest, mantling, motto: As 1.
For Sir George Chetwynd, 1st Bt., who m. 1782, Jane, dau. of Richard
Bantin of Little Faringdon, Berks, and d. 24 Mar. 1784.

7. Dexter background black

Qly, 1st and 4th, Azure a chevron between three molets or (Chetwynd),
2nd and 3rd, Argent a chevron between three annulets gules (Goring),
impaling, Barry of ten argent and azure a lion rampant gules (Stratford)
Crest: A goat's head erased proper
Mantling: Gules and argent   Motto: In caelo quies
For Henry Chetwynd, who m. Sarah, dau. and co-heir of Francis
Stratford, and d. 1755.

8. All black background

On a lozenge   Two coats per pale   Dexter, Azure a chevron
between three molets or (Chetwynd)   Sinister, Azure a lion rampant
or, on a chief or an escutcheon of Ulster (Dixie)   Both impaling, Qly,
1st and 4th, Argent a chevron between three hazel leaves vert
(Haselrigg), 2nd and 3rd, Azure a lion rampant guardant or (Brocas),
over all a crescent for cadency
For Frances, dau. of Edward Haselrigg of Arthingworth, who m. 1st,
Walter Chetwynd, and 2nd, Sir Wolston Dixie, and d. 1686.

9. All black background
Azure a chevron between three molets or (Chetwynd), impaling, Ermine two chevrons azure (Bagot)
Crest: A goat's head erased argent armed or
Mantling: Gules and argent   Motto: Moriendo vivo
For Walter Chetwynd, who m. Anne, dau. of Edward Bagot of Blithfield, and d. 1691.

HALL GREEN

1. All black background
Sable a fess dancetty ermine between three fleurs-de-lys argent (Marston)
Crest: A demi-greyhound rampant sable, collared dancetty argent
Mantling: Sable and argent   Motto: In coelo quies
For a bachelor of the Marston family of Hall Green

HANDSWORTH

1. All black background
Barry of six or and azure a club in bend sinister surmounted by a caduceus in bend proper (Watt)
Crest: On a mill-rind or an elephant proper, charged with a cross moline or
Mantling: Azure and or   Motto: Ingenio et labore
For James Watt, the inventor, who d. 1819.

HONINGTON

1. All black background
Azure a chevron ermine between three escallops argent (Townsend), impaling, Gules a fess between three cross crosslets fitchy or (Gore)
Crest: A stag trippant proper   Motto: Vita posse priore frui
For Joseph Townsend, M.P. who m. Judith, dau. and co-heir of John Gore, M.P. and d.   (B.L.G. 1871 ed.)

2. Sinister background black
Qly, 1st and 4th, Azure a chevron ermine between three escallops argent (Townsend), 2nd and 3rd, Gules a fess between three cross crosslets fitchy or (Gore), impaling, Gules a saltire argent between twelve cross crosslets or (Windsor)
Motto: Resurgam   Top of shield flanked by cherubs' heads
For Elizabeth, dau. of Other, 4th Earl of Plymouth, who m. Gore Townsend, and d. 1821.

3. All black background
Arms: As 2.
Crest: A stag trippant proper
Mantling: Gules and argent   Motto: Vita posse priore frui
For Gore Townsend, who m. Elizabeth, dau. of Other, 4th Earl of
Plymouth, and d. 1826.

4. Dexter background black
Qly, as 2, impaling, Argent an anchor erect sable between three lions'
heads erased gules, on a chief azure a portcullis chained or (Scott)
Crest: A stag statant proper
Motto: Vita posse priore frui
For Thomas Townsend, who m. Marianne, dau. of William Scott, Baron
Stowell, and d. 1820.

KINGSBURY

1. Sinister background black
Argent a chevron sable ermined argent a canton gules (?Shaw),
impaling, Qly, 1st, Gules a tower between two halberdiers respectant,
in chief a serpent argent (   ), 2nd and 3rd, Argent on a bend azure
three bezants (   ), 4th, Gules a tower between two halberdiers, in
chief a swan close argent (   )
Motto: In coelo quies
Winged cherub's head in apex of hatchment, winged half skull in base,
and pale blue cloth is draped behind shield hanging from gold brackets
Unidentified.

KINGS NORTON

1. All black background
Gules a fess between three roundels argent (Mynors)
Crest: A dexter cubit arm in armour erect holding in the hand a
lion's gamb proper
Mantling: Gules and argent   Motto: In coelo quies
Skull and cross bones in base
For Robert Mynors of Weatheroak who d. unm. 18.. (B.L.G. 1871 ed.)

2. Dexter background black
Ermine on a chief indented sable three escallops argent (Taylor),
impaling, Azure a fess ermine between three estoiles or (Skey)
Crest: A demi-lion rampant proper holding between the forepaws an
escallop or
Mantling: Gules and argent   Motto: In coelo quies
For John Taylor of Bordesley Park, who m. Sarah, dau. of Samuel Skey

of Bewdley, and d. 1814.   (B.L.G. 1871 ed.)

3. Dexter background black

Gules a fess between three roundels argent (Mynors), impaling,
Gules on a chevron argent between three garbs or three roundels azure
(Eden)
Crest: A dexter cubit arm in armour erect, holding in the hand a lion's
gamb proper
Mantling: Gules and argent   Motto: In coelo quies
For Robert Mynors of Weatheroak, Worcs, who m. Susannah, dau. of
Thomas Eden, and d. 1806. (B.L.G. 1871 ed.)

4. Dexter background black

Taylor, with Skey in pretence, as 2., impaling, Qly, 1st and 4th,
Sable a chevron between three millpicks argent (Moseley), 2nd, Qly per
fess indented sable and argent in the 1st qr a lion passant guardant or
(Croft), 3rd, Gules two lions passant argent between nine cross crosslets
fitchy or, three, three and three (Acton)
Crest: A demi-lion rampant ermine holding between its paws an
escallop or
Mantling: Gules and argent   Motto: Fidelisque ad mortem
For James Taylor of Moseley Hall, who m. 1st, 1814, Louisa, 2nd
dau. and co-heir of Samuel Skey, of Spring Grove, Worcs. She d. 1822.
He m. 2nd, 1825, Anne Elizabeth, dau. of Walter Michael Moseley of
Buildwas Park, Salop, and d. 8 Oct. 1852. (B.L.G. 1871 ed.)
(There is a duplicate of this hatchment in the parish church of
Strensham, Worcs.)

LITTLE WOLFORD MANOR

1. Sinister background black

Qly, 1st and 4th, Per pale azure and sable semy-de-lys argent a lion
rampant holding a mascle or, a canton ermine (Philips), 2nd and 3rd,
Gules on a plain bend cotised engrailed between two pheons or three
stags' heads cabossed gules (Stubbs), over all the Badge of Ulster,
impaling, Qly, as dexter, but without Badge
For Sarah Ann, dau. of Nathaniel Philips, who m. 1788, George Philips
(cr. a baronet 1828) and d. 2 Sept. 1844.

2. All black background

Qly, as 1. with Badge of Ulster, but no impalement
Crest: A demi-lion rampant or ermined sable, between the paws a
mascle or
No mantling or motto
For Sir George Philips, 1st Bt., who m. 1788, Sarah Ann, dau. of
Nathaniel Philips, and d. 3rd Oct. 1847.

3. Dexter background black

Qly, 1st and 4th, Ermine on a fess gules three escallops or (Ingram), 2nd and 3rd, Azure a lion rampant or a chief gules (   )   In pretence: Ermine a millrind sable (Mills)   Also impaling, Per pale or and gules a cross formy fitchy counterchanged (Clopton)
Crest: An eagle's head couped qly gules and argent beaked or
Unidentified

MANCETTER

1. Sinister background black

Vairy argent and sable a fess gules (Bracebridge), impaling, Sable a fess or fretty sable between three fleurs-de-lys or (Stiles)
Two cherubs' heads above shield, and winged skull below
For Mary, dau. of John Stiles of Uxbridge, who m. Abraham Bracebridge, and d. c. 1760. (B.L.G. 1871 ed.)

2. Sinister background black

Ermine on a chief gules three bezants (Okeover), impaling, Or a chevron between in chief two roses gules barbed and seeded proper and in base a dolphin embowed proper (Langston)
Motto: In coelo quies A lover's knot between two cherubs' heads above shield which is flanked by branches
For Bridget, dau. of James Haughton Langston of London, who m. Rowland Farmer Okeover, of Oldbury Hall, and d.c. 1790. (B.L.G. 1871 ed.)

3. All black background

Argent a bear salient sable muzzled or (Barnard), impaling, Azure a chevron between three ?chanfrons or (   )
Crest: A demi-bear salient sable muzzled or
Mantling: Gules and argent
Frame decorated with skulls and cross bones   A very small hatchment, c. 20" x 20"
Unidentified

MAXSTOKE

1. Sinister background black

Qly, 1st and 4th, Gules a lion rampant per pale argent and or (Dilke), 2nd and 3rd, Argent a molet sable, in dexter chief a martlet gules for difference (Ashton), impaling, Argent a lion rampant within a bordure gules (Russell)
Motto: Mors janua vitae

For Anne, dau. of Charles Russell of Thetford, Norfolk, who m. William
Dilke of Maxstoke, and d. 1749.   (B.L.G. 1871 ed.)

2. All black background
Gules a lion rampant per pale or and argent (Dilke), impaling, Argent a
lion rampant within a bordure gules (Russell)
Crest: A dove argent beaked and membered gules
Mantling: Gules and argent   Motto: Mors janua vitae   Skull in base
For William Dilke, who m. Anne, dau. of Charles Russell of Thetford,
Norfolk, and d. 1753.

3. Dexter background black
Gules a lion rampant per pale argent and or, a label argent for
difference (Dilke), impaling, Argent a cross moline gules charged with
a king of arms' coronet or, in the first quarter a roundel gules
(Dugdale)
Crest and mantling: As 2.   No motto
For William Dilke, who m. Louisa Anna, dau. of Richard Geast Dugdale,
and d. 1797.

4. All black background
On a lozenge
Dilke, as 3., impaling, Qly, 1st and 4th, Dugdale, as 3., 2nd and 3rd,
Barry of ten argent and azure a lion rampant gules (Stratford)
For Louisa Anna, dau. of Richard Geast Dugdale, who m. William
Dilke, of Maxstoke, and d. 1849.

5. All black background
Dilke as 3.
Crest: As 2.
Mantling: Gules and argent   Motto: Resurgam
Possibly for William Dilke, d. unm. 18 . .

MEREVALE

1. All black background
Qly, 1st and 4th, Or on a chevron vert three leopards faces argent (Inge),
2nd and 3rd, Azure on a chevron engrailed between three lions passant
guardant or three crosses moline sable (Fowler), impaling, Fowler
Crest: Two battleaxes in saltire proper enfiled with a ducal coronet or
Mantling: Gules and argent   Motto: Ne cede malis
For Richard Inge of Shrewsbury, who m. Mary, dau. of Thomas Fowler
of Pendeford, and d. 1784.   (B.L.G. 1871 ed)

2. Dexter background black
A shield and a lozenge
Shield: Qly, 1st and 4th, Argent a cross flory gules charged with a king

of arms coronet or, in the first quarter a roundel gules (Dugdale), 2nd
and 3rd, Barry of ten argent and azure a lion rampant gules (Stratford),
impaling two coats per pale; dexter, Qly, 1st and 4th, Argent on a bend
sable three popinjays or collared gules (Curzon), 2nd and 3rd, Argent
two lions passant guardant azure (Hanmer), and sinister, Argent a lion
rampant gules between three pheons sable (Egerton)   Lozenge: Qly,
1st and 4th, Argent a chevron sable between three fountains proper
(Sykes), 2nd and 3rd, Gules three fleurs-de-lys or (Masterman), over
all the Badge of Ulster, impaling, Argent a lion rampant gules between
three pheons sable (Egerton)
Crests: Dexter, A griffin's head wings endorsed and gorged with a
coronet as in the arms or (Dugdale)   Sinister, An arm embowed
habited argent, in the hand proper a scimitar or (Stratford)
Mantling: Gules and argent   Motto: Pestis pegrities patria
For Dugdale Stratford Dugdale, who m. 1st, Charlotte, dau. of
Assheton, Viscount Curzon, and 2nd, Mary Elizabeth, dau. of
Wilbraham Tatton Egerton, widow of Sir Mark Masterman Sykes, 3rd
Bt, and d. 5 Nov. 1836.   (B.P. 1938 ed)

3. Sinister background black
Qly, Dugdale and Stratford, as 2., impaling Curzon, as 2.
Motto: Resurgam   Cherub's head above shield
For Charlotte, dau. of Assheton, Viscount Curzon, 1st wife of Dugdale
Stratford Dugdale.   She d. 30 Dec. 1832.

4. All black background
On a lozenge
Barry azure and argent a lion rampant gules (Stratford), impaling,
Qly sable and or in the dexter chief a cinquefoil or (Packe)
Motto: In coelo quies
Cherub's head above lozenge and skull and crossbones below
For Anna, dau. of Clifton Packe of Prestwold, and widow of Francis
Stratford.   She d. 1762.   (B.L.G. 1871 ed.)

5. Dexter background black
Stratford impaling Packe, as 4., but cinquefoil argent
Crest: An arm embowed in armour proper, in the hand a scimitar argent
hilted or
Mantling: Gules and argent   Motto: Mors janua vitae
Skull and crossbones below shield
For Francis Stratford, who m. Anna, dau. of Clifton Packe of
Prestwold, and d. 1762.

MILVERTON

1. ?Dexter background black
Sable on a cross quarter-pierced argent four eagles displayed sable, in
the dexter chief a molet argent charged with a crescent or for cadency
(Buller), impaling, Argent a saltire engrailed gules (Lynd)
Crest: A Saracen's head and shoulders affronté couped proper
Mantling: Gules and argent   Motto: Aquila non capit muscas
For the Rev. Arthur Buller, who m. Grace, dau. of Charles Lynd, of
Mullantaine House, co. Tyrone, and d. 30 Nov. 1850.

MONKS KIRBY

1. All black background
Argent three bars gules in chief a greyhound courant sable collared or
(Skipwith), impaling, Paly of six or and azure a canton ermine (Shirley),
at fess point of shield the Badge of Ulster
Crest: A turnstile proper   Motto: Sans dieu je ne puis
For Sir Thomas George Skipwith, 4th Bt., who m. Selina, dau. of
George Shirley, and d.s.p. 1790.   (B.E.B.)

PACKWOOD

1. All black background
Gules on a chevron between three ostrich feathers argent three roundels
gules (Fetherston), impaling, Azure a lion rampant and a chief or
(Dixie)
Crest: An antelope's head gules armed and crined or
Mantling: Gules and argent   Motto: In spe salutis
For Charles Fetherston (formerly Dilke) who m. 1814, Elizabeth, dau.
of the Rev. Beaumont Dixie, Rector of Newton Blossomville, and d. 26
Mar. 1832.   (B.L.G. 1871 ed.)

PRESTON-ON-STOUR

1. All black background
On a lozenge surmounted by a cherub's head
Qly, 1st and 4th, Argent a fess dancetty sable (West), 2nd and 3rd,
Or on a chevron between three demi-lions gules three cross crosslets or
(Steavens)
For Henrietta, dau. of James West of Alscot.   She d. unm. 1815.
(B.L.G. 1871 ed)

2. All black background

On a lozenge surmounted by a winged cherub's head
West, as 1.   In pretence: Steavens as 1. but cross crosslets argent
For Sarah, dau. of Sir Thomas Steavens of Eltham, Kent, who m. James
West of Alscot, and d. 1799.

3. Dexter background black

Qly, 1st and 4th, Argent a fess dancetty sable ermined argent (West), 2nd,
Or on a chevron gules between three demi-lions rampant sable three
cross crosslets argent (Steavens), 3rd, Argent three pheons sable, on a
chief sable a greyhound courant argent (Roberts), impaling, Gules two
arrows in saltire or barbed argent between two bezants in pale
(Boultbee)
Crest: Out of a ducal coronet or a griffin's head sable ermined or
beaked or   No mantling   Motto: Dux vitae ratio
For James Roberts-West, of Alscot Park, who m. 1844, Elizabeth, dau.
of Joseph M. Boultbee, of Springfield House, Knowle, and d. 6 Feb.
1882.   (B.L.G. 1871 ed)

4. Dexter background black

Qly, 1st and 4th, Argent a fess dancetty sable, a martlet sable for
difference (West), 2nd and 3rd, Steavens, as 2.   In pretence:
Argent three pheons sable, on a chief sable a greyhound courant proper
(Roberts)
Crest: Out of a ducal coronet or a griffin's head azure beaked or
Mantling: Gules and argent   Motto: Dux vitae ratio
For James Roberts-West, of Alscot Park, who m. Anne, dau. and heir
of Joseph Roberts, of Newcombe, Gloucs, and d. 25 Mar. 1838.

SNITTERFIELD

1. Dexter background black

Qly, 1st and 4th, Sable a fess ermine between three crescents or
(Coventry), 2nd, Argent a fess between six cross crosslets gules
(Craven), 3rd, Or five fleurs-de-lys in cross sable, a chief wavy azure
(Craven ancient), impaling, Qly France and England, within a bordure
compony argent and azure (Beaufort)
Earl's coronet   Crest: On a garb fesswise a dunghill cock gules
Mantling: Gules and ermine   Motto: Candide et constanter
Supporters: Dexter, An eagle, wings expanded inverted argent,
beaked or   Sinister, A panther argent semy of roundels gules,
azure and vert, flames issuing from the ears and mouth proper,
gorged with a plain collar and chained or
For Thomas, 2nd Earl of Coventry, who m. Anne, dau. of Henry, Duke
of Beaufort, and d. Aug. 1710.

2. All black background
On a lozenge surmounted by a countess's coronet   Coventry, as 1.,
impaling, Beaufort, as 1.
Supporters and motto: as 1., but eagle proper and panther lined or
Skull and crossbones in base
For Anne, dau. of Henry, Duke of Beaufort, who m. Thomas, 2nd Earl
of Coventry, and d. 17 Feb. 1763.

SOLIHULL

1. All black background
Qly, 1st and 4th, Argent on a bend sable five bezants (Palmer), 2nd and
3rd, Sable a chevron between three crescents argent (Palmer), impaling,
Argent a fess gules in chief two greyhounds courant in pale sable
(Greswolde)
Crest: A wyvern or wings lined gules
Mantling: Gules and argent
For Henry Palmer, of Olton End, who m. Ann, dau. of Humphrey
Greswolde, and d.   (B.L.G. 1848 ed.)

2. All black background
Argent a fess gules in chief two greyhounds courant in pale sable
(Greswolde)
Crest: A cubit arm erect thereon a hawk proper
Mantling: Gules and argent   Motto: Spes incerta futuri
For Lieut. Colonel Edmund Meysey Wigley, who assumed the name of
Greswolde, and d. unm. in 1833.   (B.L.G. 1848 ed.)

3. All black background
On a lozenge
Argent a fess gules in chief two greyhounds courant in pale sable
(Greswolde)
Unidentified

4. All black background
Qly, 1st and 4th, Sable a chevron between three crescents argent
(Palmer), 2nd and 3rd, Argent a ? cockatrice (four legs) sable, beaked,
combed, wattled and legged or (Grimshaw), impaling, Argent three
pallets within a bordure engrailed gules, on a canton gules a spur
leathered or (Knight)
Crest: A wyvern or
Mantling: Gules and argent
For Benjamin Palmer, who m. Elizabeth, dau. of Edward Knight of
Wolverley, and d.   (B.L.G. 1871 ed.)

SOUTHAM

1. Dexter background black
Qly, 1st and 4th, Or on a mount vert a tree proper between on the
dexter a human heart gules and on the sinister a falcon close proper,
belled or, in chief two molets sable (Fauquier), 2nd and 3rd, Gules an
escutcheon argent within an orle of eight molets or (Chamberlayne)
Crest: A falcon close proper belled or
Mantling: Gules and argent   Motto: Resurgam
For Francis Fauquier, who m. Thermutis, dau. of Stanes Chamberlayne,
and d. 1804/5. She d.s.p. 1822. (per College of Arms)

2. All black background
On a lozenge surmounted by a cherub's head
Qly, 1st and 4th, Fauquier, 2nd and 3rd, Chamberlayne, as 1.   In
pretence: Qly, 1st and 4th, Chamberlayne, 2nd and 3rd, Azure three
bends or (   )
Motto: Resurgam
Unidentified

3. All black background
Qly, 1st and 4th, Azure three millpicks or (Packwood), 2nd and 3rd,
Sable three bells argent a canton argent (Porter), impaling, Argent on a
bend between two lions rampant sable a wyvern volant argent (Rudinge)
Crest: A demi-lion rampant holding between the forepaws a bell sable
charged with a canton ermine (Porter)
Mantling: Gules and argent
Motto: None is truly great but he that is truly good
Unidentified

STIVICHALL

1. Dexter background black
Or two bars and in chief a lion passant azure (Gregory), impaling,
Azure a fret argent on a chief or three crescents sable (Hood)
Crest: A demi-boar sable, unguled, tusked, bristled and collared or
Mantling: Azure and argent   Motto: Vigilanter
Supporters: Dexter, A lion rampant argent crowned or   Sinister, A
boar sable, unguled, tusked, bristled and collared or
For Arthur Francis Gregory of Stivichall, who m. Caroline, sister of
Samuel, 3rd Viscount Hood, and d. 1853. (B.L.G. 1871 ed.)

2. Dexter background black
Qly of six, 1st, Or two bars and in chief a lion passant azure (Gregory),
2nd, Sable, a lion rampant argent debruised by a bendlet gules (Segrave),
3rd, Ermine a fess paly of six or and gules (Malyn), 4th, Sable two lions

passant guardant argent crowned or (Ludlow), 6th Vair a fess gules
fretty or (Marmion), impaling, Argent on a mount vert three pine trees
proper, a dexter side or (Grote)
Crest: A demi-boar sable, tusked, bristled and collared or
Mantling: Gules and argent   Motto: Vigilanter
For Francis Gregory of Stivichall, who m. Frances, dau. of Andrew
Grote, and d. 1833.

STONELEIGH

1. Dexter background black
Gules a cross engrailed in dexter chief a lozenge argent (Leigh) In
pretence and impaling, Vert six escallops three two and one or (Holbeche)
Baron's coronet
Crest: An unicorn's head couped argent, armed and crined or
Mantling: Gules and argent   Motto: Tout vient de dieu
Supporters: Two unicorns rampant or
For Edward, 3rd Baron Leigh, who m. Mary, dau. and heir of Thomas
Holbeche of Fillongley, and d. 9 Mar. 1737/38. (B.E.B.)

2. All black background
Or a cross engrailed in dexter chief a lozenge argent (Leigh)
Baron's coronet
Crest, motto and supporters: As 1. but unicorns argent, armed etc. or
Mantle: Gules and ermine
Winged skull wearing an ancient crown in apex of hatchment
Probably, for Edward, 5th Baron Leigh, who d. unm. 26 Mar. 1786.

3. All black background
Gules a cross engrailed in dexter chief a lozenge argent (Leigh),
impaling, Argent on a chevron engrailed azure between three martlets
sable three crescents or (Watson)   Baron's coronet
Crest: An unicorn's head erased or
Mantling: Gules and argent   Motto: Tout vient de dieu
Supporters: Dexter, A unicorn rampant or   Sinister, A griffin segreant
argent ducally gorged or
For Thomas, 2nd Baron Leigh, who m. 2nd, Eleanor, dau. of Edward,
2nd Lord Rockingham, and d. 1710.

4. Sinister background black
Arms, coronet, crest, mantling and motto: As 3.
Supporters: Two unicorns rampant or
For Eleanor, wife of Thomas, 2nd Baron Leigh. She d. 17..

5. All black background
Gules a cross engrailed and in dexter chief a lozenge or a crescent for

cadency (Leigh), impaling, Gules a cross engrailed and in dexter chief a
lozenge or (Leigh)
Crest: An unicorn's head erased or
No mantling or motto
Shield flanked by flowering branches, tied at the base with a gold ribbon
For the Rev. Thomas Leigh, who m. his cousin, Mary dau. of Theophilus
Leigh, and d. 1806.   (Burke's Commoners 1836)

6. All black background

On a lozenge surmounted by a cherub's head   Gules a cross engrailed
argent in dexter chief a lozenge or (Leigh)
Motto: Resurgam
Possibly for Mary, sister and heir of Edward, 5th Baron Leigh. She d.
2 July 1806.

7. Dexter background black

Gules a cross engrailed and in dexter chief a lozenge or (Leigh), impaling,
Or a chevron between three moles proper (Twisleton)
Crest: An unicorn's head erased argent armed and crined or
Mantling: Gules and argent   Motto: Tout vient de dieu
Cherub's head on each side of shield
For James Henry Leigh, who m. Julia Judith, dau. of Thomas, Lord
Saye and Sele, and d. 27 Oct. 1823.   (B.P. 1938 ed.)
(There is a duplicate of this hatchment in the parish church at
Adlestrop, Gloucs.)

8. All black background

On a lozenge surmounted by a cherub's head
Gules a cross engrailed and in dexter chief a lozenge argent (Leigh),
impaling, Qly, 1st and 3rd, Argent a chevron between three moles
sable (Twisleton), 2nd, Argent a bear sejant sable a canton ermine
(Bere), 4th, Azure three lions rampant or (Fiennes), 5th, Qly or and
gules (Saye), 6th, Argent two chevronels sable between three roses
gules (Wykeham)
For Julia Judith, dau. of Thomas, Lord Saye and Sele, and widow of
James Henry Leigh. She d. 8 Feb. 1843.

9. Dexter background black

Gules a cross engrailed in dexter chief a lozenge argent (Leigh),
impaling, Qly, 1st and 4th, Argent a chevron sable between three molets
gules (Willes), 2nd and 3rd, Or on a fess azure between three Cornish
choughs sable three crescents or, in chief a spearhead proper (Williams)
Baron's coronet
Crest: An unicorn's head erased or
No mantle   Motto: Tout vient de dieu
Supporters: Two unicorns rampant or, each gorged with a ducal coronet
gules, pendant therefrom an escutcheon charged with the arms of

Brydges, Argent on a cross sable a leopard's face or
For Chandos, 1st Baron Leigh, who m. Margarette, dau. of the Rev.
William Shippen Willes of Northants, and d. 27 Sept. 1850.
(The hatchment of his widow is in the parish church at Adlestrop,
Gloucs.)

STRATFORD-ON-AVON

1. All black background
Qly, 1st and 4th, Per pale or and gules a cross formy counterchanged
(Clopton), 2nd and 3rd, Paly of four or and azure a lion rampant
counterchanged (Cokefield)   In pretence: Qly, 1st, Argent a chevron
ringed at the point between three crescents sable (Walker), 2nd and
3rd, Argent on a cross gules five leopards' faces or (   ), 4th, Azure
a cross lozenge ermine (   )
Crest: An eagle displayed wings inverted standing on a tun or (N.B. The crest
crest is not in its normal position; there is no helm, and the crest wreath is
in the base of the hatchment; the tun and the eagle occupy the whole of
the hatchment, the eagle appearing as a single supporter behind the shield)
Mantling: None   Motto: Loyaute mon honneur
For Sir John Clopton, who m. Barbara, dau. and heir of Sir Edward
Walker, and d. 18 Apr. 1719.

2. All black background
Qly Clopton and Cokefield, as 1.   In pretence; Ermine on a fess gules
three bezants (Milward)
Crest: An eagle wings displayed and inverted standing upon a tun or
Mantling: None   Motto: Loyaute mon honneur
Two small shields flank main shield   Dexter, Clopton quartering
Cokefield, impaling Milward   Sinister, Clopton quartering
Cokefield, impaling, Gules three boys' heads couped at the shoulders
proper crined or (   )
For Sir Hugh Clopton, who m. 1st, Elizabeth, dau. of Thomas Milward,
and 2nd, Elizabeth, widow of Daniel Smith, and d. 1751.

3. Dexter background black
Qly, 1st and 4th, Vairy argent and sable on a chief sable three roses
argent (Partheriche), 2nd and 3rd, Gules on a chevron argent three bars
gemel sable (Throckmorton)   In pretence: Qly, 1st and 4th, Clopton,
2nd, Walker, 3rd Cokefield, all as 1.
Crest: A dexter arm in armour embowed holding a fireball inflamed proper
Mantling: Gules and argent   Motto: In coelo quies
For John Partheriche of Alderminster, who m. Frances, dau. of Edward
Clopton of Clopton, and d. 1783.

4. All black background
On a cartouche   Qly, 1st and 4th, Partheriche, 2nd and 3rd,
Throckmorton   In pretence: Qly, 1st and 4th, Clopton, 2nd, Walker,
3rd, Cokefield, all as 3.
For Frances, dau. of Edward Clopton of Clopton, who m. John
Partheriche of Alderminster, and d. 1792.

STUDLEY

1. All black background
Argent a cross engrailed in dexter chief a ducal coronet gules
(Knottisford)
Crest: An eagle displayed or
Mantle: Gules and argent   No motto
Probably for John Knottisford, who d. 1781. (Tomb in churchyard)

TEMPLE BALSALL

1. All black background
On a lozenge   Azure three leaves or (Leveson), impaling, Or a lion
rampant double-queued vert, charged on the shoulder with a crescent
argent (Dudley)
For Catherine, dau. of Sir Robert Dudley, who m. Sir Richard Leveson,
K.B. and d.

WARWICK

1. Sinister background black
Argent two chevrons and a bordure engrailed sable (Staunton),
impaling, Qly, 1st and 4th, Azure a ?grapnel argent (?Standert), 2nd,
Gules three pears or on a chief argent a demi-lion issuant sable
(Perrott), 3rd, Paly of six or and gules on a chief azure three lions
rampant or (Bonner)
Mantling: Gules and argent
Three cherubs' heads above shield
For Elizabeth, dau. of Osborne Standert, of London, who m. William
Staunton of Longbridge, and d. 1835. (B.L.G. 1871 ed.)

2. All black background
Staunton, impaling, Qly, 1st and 4th, ?Standert, 2nd, Perrott, 3rd,
Bonner, as 1.
Crest: A fox statant proper
Mantling: Gules and argent   Motto: En dieu ma foy
For William Staunton of Longbridge, who m. Elizabeth, dau. of

Osborne Standert of London, and d. 1848.

3. Dexter background black
Qly, 1st and 4th, Sable on a cross engrailed or five roundels sable,
within a bordure engrailed or (Greville), 2nd, Azure fretty or
(Willoughby), 3rd, Gules a fess between six cross crosslets or
(Beauchamp), impaling, to the dexter, Azure a lion rampant queue-
fourché ermine crowned or, on a canton or a molet gules pierced or
(Peachey), and to the sinister, Qly, 1st and 4th, Argent a fret sable
(Vernon), 2nd and 3rd, Or on a fess azure three garbs or (Vernon)
Earl's coronet   Crests: Dexter, Out of a ducal coronet or a demi-
swan wings expanded argent beaked gules   Sinister, A bear erect
supporting a staff raguly argent
Mantle: Gules and ermine   Motto: Vix ea nostra voco
Supporters: Two swans wings addorsed argent ducally gorged gules
For George Greville, 2nd Earl of Warwick, who m. 1st, 1771, Georgiana,
dau. of James, 1st Lord Selsey, and 2nd, 1776, Henrietta, dau. of
Richard Vernon, and d. 1816. (B.P. 1938 ed.)

4. Exactly as 3.

5. All black background
On a lozenge
Qly, 1st and 4th, Greville, 2nd, Willoughby, 3rd, Beauchamp, as 3.,
impaling, Qly, 1st and 4th, Argent a fret sable (Vernon), 2nd and 3rd,
Or on a fess azure three garbs or (Vernon)
Countess's coronet
Supporters: Two swans wings addorsed argent ducally gorged gules
For Henrietta, dau. of Richard Vernon, 2nd wife of George, 2nd Earl
of Warwick, She d. 1838.

6. Sinister background black
Qly, 1st and 4th, Greville, 2nd Willoughby, 3rd, Beauchamp,
as 3., impaling, Qly, 1st and 4th, Argent on a bend sable
three owls argent (Savile), 2nd, Gules a cross formy or (   ), 3rd,
Argent a bend sable between in chief an eagle displayed vert and in
base a cross crosslet fitchy gules (Rushworth)
Countess's coronet   Supporters: Dexter, a swan wings addorsed argent
ducally gorged gules   Sinister, A lion or collared and chained azure
the collar charged with three crescents argent
For Sarah Elizabeth, dau. of John, 2nd Earl of Mexborough, who m.
Henry Richard, 3rd Earl of Warwick, and d. 30 Jan. 1851.
(There is a duplicate of this hatchment in the parish church at
Gatton, Surrey)

7. All black background
Arms, as 6.

Earl's coronet   Crests: As 3. but bear muzzled gules   Motto: Vix
ea nostra voco
Supporters: As 6.
Issuing from behind the coronet is a scroll inscribed with the motto of
the Order of the Thistle, and above it is the Badge of the Order
For Henry Richard, 3rd Earl of Warwick, K.T., who m. Sarah Elizabeth,
dau. of John, 2nd Earl of Mexborough, and d. 10 Aug. 1853.

WISHAW

1. Dexter background black

Sable three piles in point argent on a chief argent a lion passant gules
(Hacket), impaling, Argent on a bend azure three mascles argent
(Adderley)
Crest: An eagle's head erased proper
Mantling: Gules and argent   Motto: Fides sufficit
For Andrew Hacket of Moxhull, who m. Letitia Penelope, dau. of
Ralph Adderley of Coton, and d. 1815.   (B.L.G. 1871 ed.)

2. All black background

On a lozenge   Qly, 1st and 4th, Or fretty gules a canton ermine (Noel),
2nd and 3rd, Per fess or and gules a lion rampant within a double
tressure flory-counter-flory, all counterchanged (Middleton), impaling,
Qly, 1st, Argent on a bend azure three mascles argent (Adderley), 2nd,
Argent a lion rampant between three cross crosslets fitchy gules
(Bowyer), 3rd, Ermine a fess chequy or and azure (Arden), 4th, Azure
a lion rampant within an orle of cross crosslets or (Kynnersley)
Mantling: Gules and argent   Motto: In coelo quies
For Letitia Penelope, dau. of Ralph Adderley of Coton, who m. 2nd,
the Hon. Berkeley Octavius Noel, and d. 1860.

WOLSTON

1. All black background

Argent a chevron engrailed gules between three cocks' heads erased
sable, combed and wattled gules(   ), impaling, Or a lion rampant
gules between eight spearheads azure (   )
Crest: (no helm) A doubleheaded eagle displayed argent beaked and
legged or
Mantling: None   Motto Vigilans et audax
Unidentified

WOOTTON WAWEN

1. All black background

Or ermined sable a lion rampant sable ducally gorged and chained or
between two cross crosslets fitchy in chief and an escallop in base gules
(Phillips)   In pretence: Or on a fess azure three garbs or in chief a
cross crosslet fitchy gules (Vernon)   Also impaling, Azure a fess or
ermined sable between three molets or in chief and a crescent in base
argent (Weir)
Crest: On a garb fesswise or a lion rampant sable ducally gorged and
chained or, between the paws a cross crosslet fitchy or
Mantling: Gules and argent   Motto: Ducit amor patriae
For John Phillips of Edstone, who m. 1st, Emma, dau. and heir of
Thomas Vernon of Hanbury, Worcs, and 2nd, Mary, dau. of Robert
Weir of Hall Craig, co.Fermanagh, and d. 1836.

2. Dexter background black

Qly, 1st and 4th, Argent three bendlets gules on a canton azure a spur
rowel downwards, leathered or (Knight), 2nd and 3rd, qly i. & iv. Gules
a lion rampant reguardant or (Powell), ii. & iii. Argent three bears'
heads couped sable (Powell), impaling, Qly, 1st and 4th, Per chevron
embattled sable and argent, in chief two estoiles or and in base a
heathcock proper (Heath), 2nd and 3rd, Argent on a fess between
three martlets gules three bezants (Bayley)
Crest: A spur rowel upwards, leathered or between two wings displayed
gules
Mantling: Gules and argent   Motto: Te digna sequere
Supporters: Dexter, A lion rampant reguardant or   Sinister, A boar
rampant sable ducally gorged and chained or
For Henry Knight, Viscount Barrels, who m. Frances, dau. of Thomas
Heath of Stanstead, Essex, and d. 1762.

3. Dexter background black

Qly, 1st and 4th, Argent a cross gules between four peacocks azure
(Carington), 2nd and 3rd, Argent on a bend vert six falchions saltire-
wise argent hilted or (Carington), impaling, Barry of six gules and
argent on a chief or a lion passant azure (Englefield)
Crest: A peacock's head erased azure ducally gorged or
Mantling: Gules and argent   Motto: Regi semper fidelis
For Francis Smith Carington, who m. Mary, dau. of Sir Henry
Englefield, of White Knights, and d. 1749.

4. All black background

Qly, 1st and 4th, qly, i. Azure an oak tree argent (Duroure),ii. Or a
lion rampant vair crowned azure (   ), iii. Gules a chief indented or
(   ), iv. Or two lions passant guardant azure (   ), v. Argent a
tower gules (   ), vi. Sable a lion rampant within a bordure engrailed

argent (   ), 2nd , Argent three bendlets gules on a canton azure a
spur leathered or (Knight of Barrels), 3rd, Qly, i. & iv. Gules a lion
rampant reguardant or (Powell), ii & iii. Argent three boars' heads
couped sable langued gules (Powell)
Crest: Dexter, From a ducal coronet sable a mermaid proper rising
from a bath or   Sinister, A spur erect leathered or between two
wings displayed argent
Mantle: Gules and argent   Motto: Vetus state robur
Supporters: Two angels proper (dexter, winged or habited azure;
sinister, winged argent habited gules) each holding in the outer hand a
banner, the dexter bearing, Gules a chief indented or, and the sinister,
Sable a lion rampant within a bordure engrailed argent
Unidentified

WROXALL

1. All black background

Argent a chevron between three lions' heads erased azure, on a chief
gules three cross crosslets or (Wren), impaling, to the dexter, Gules on
a chevron argent three roundels sable, a chief sable (Coghill), and to
the sinister, Lozengy argent and gules (Fitzwilliam)
Crest: A lion's head erased azure pierced through the neck with a spear
or
Mantling: Gules and argent   Motto: Numero pondere et mensura
For Sir Christopher Wren, the architect of St. Paul's Cathedral, who
m. 1st, Faith, dau. of Sir Thomas Coghill, and 2nd, Jane, dau. of
William Fitzwilliam, and d. 1723.   (Mural monument in church)

YARDLEY

1. All black background

Two coats per pale   Dexter, Qly, 1st and 4th, Gules three serpents
in triangle or within a bordure engrailed or (Lewis), 2nd and 3rd,
Argent a fess gules in chief two greyhounds courant sable (Greswolde)
Sinister, Qly, 1st and 4th, Azure semy of roses a lion rampant or
(   ), 2nd and 3rd, Sable a wolf rampant argent (   ), both impaling,
Sable ten roundels four, three, two and one argent, on a chief argent
a lion passant sable (Bridgeman)
Crest: On a clenched fist erect a hawk proper belled or
Mantling: Gules and argent   Motto: In Christo salus
For Henry Greswolde Lewis, of Malvern Hall, Warws, who m. Charlotte,
dau. of Henry, 1st Baron Bradford, and d. 1829.   (B.P. 1938 ed)

PACKWOOD HOUSE

1. Dexter background black

Sable three salmon hauriant argent (Salmond), impaling, Qly gules and
vair a bend or (Constable)
Crest: A dexter arm embowed grasping a trident or
Mantling: Gules and argent   Motto: Optima sapientia probitas
For Major-General James Hanson Salmond, who m. 2nd, 1808, Rachel
Mary Ann, dau. of the Ven. Thomas Constable of Beverley, and d.
1 Nov. 1827.   (B.L.G. 1871 ed.)

2. Dexter background black

Barry of six azure and or three escutcheons ermine (for Mascall),
impaling, Argent a chevron between three bulls heads cabossed sable
(Curteis)
Crest: A sealion proper   Mantling: Gules and argent
Motto: Spero in Deo
For Robert Mascall of Ashford, who m. Martha, dau. of Jeremiah
Curteis of Tenterden, and d. 1815.

3. Dexter background black

Qly, 1st, Or a lion rampant proper (   ), 2nd Argent three fleurs-de-lys
or (   ), 3rd, Argent a double headed eagle displayed or (   ), 4th, Or
a bearded head affronté couped proper, wreathed azure (   ), impaling
to dexter, Argent on a chevron azure between three pink roses
stalked and leaved proper three fleurs-de-lys argent (?Cope), and to
sinister, Azure two lions passant argent ?vulned gules (?Strangeways)
Crest: A lion rampant or   Motto: Resurgam
Unidentified
A very poorly, and certainly inaccurately, painted hatchment.

4. Dexter background black

Two shields   Dexter, Qly, 1st, Or a goat sable within a bordure
compony or and sable (Cabrera), 2nd, Or three escallops argent (   ),
3rd, Or a leafless tree eradicated sable (   ), 4th, Or six bendlets
sinister gules, on a chief argent three roundels gules (   ) In pretence:
Argent a tree proper, on a chief gules a fish naiant or (   )
Sinister, Argent a cross flory between four Cornish cloughs proper
(Richards) Behind the shields are two batons crossed in saltire, that
from the dexter gules charged with towers or, that from the sinister
argent charged with lions rampant gules
All on a mantle gules and ermine surmounted by a count's coronet or
For Ramon de Cabrera, Comte de Moralla of Spain, who m. Marianna
Catherine, dau. of Robert Vaughan Richards, of Croft House, co.
Pembroke, and d. 18 . .   (B.L.G. 1871 ed.)

WORCESTERSHIRE

Norton-with-Lenchwick (No. 1): For Sir William Craven, 1655

INTRODUCTION

In his Heraldry of Worcestershire (1873), Grazebrook lists more than sixteen hundred armigerous families. It seems certain that there were originally many more hatchments than the sixty-seven which now remain; neglect, decay and Victorian restoration must have been responsible for considerable losses. There are also two examples of diamond-shaped boards bearing coats of arms, which are not true hatchments in that they lack the characteristic background and bear memorial inscriptions. The one at Eldersfield records the death of William Underhill in 1647, and the other at Upton, Henry Bromley who died in the same year.

The earliest hatchment in the county is for Sir William Craven, 1655, at Norton-with-Lenchwick; here also can be seen his funeral 'Hachements', helmet, crest, surcoat, sword, gauntlets and spurs. The only other seventeenth century hatchment is at Kidderminster, for Henry Gorges, 1658; this is more typical of the period, being small (c.2ft. x 2ft.) and painted on a wood panel. There are six eighteenth century examples, the earliest being for Francis Taylor D.D. of South Littleton, 1722.

All the other hatchments probably belong to the nineteenth century (some remain unidentified), and these vary in quality from the finely painted one at Bayton to the crude and obviously country product for Noel of Bell Hall. An interesting example is that for Mary, Marchioness of Downshire, 1836, at Ombersley, showing arms on two lozenges with coronets and supporters. The latest is for Marcus Brown-Westhead, 1897, at Wolverley.

An unusual non-heraldic feature in the form of an angel supporting the shield appears on the hatchment of Mary, wife of Charles Michael Berington, at Little Malvern.

83

There is a coloured illustration of a fine hatchment in Volume 2 of Thomas Habington's A Survey of Worcestershire (Worcs. Hist. Soc. 1899), depicting the twelve quarterings of Habington impaling the twenty-four quarterings of Parker. This was used at the funeral of Thomas Habington, the county historian, in 1647, but no trace of it has been found.

It is with much pleasure that I acknowledge the work of my son, Mr Richard Peplow, who photographed every hatchment and helped in the recording, and also the assistance of the late Mr G.A. Harrison in checking blazons and identifications.

W.A. Peplow
Wych Garth, Dingle Road, Pedmore, Stourbridge

ARLEY

1. All black background
Qly, 1st, Paly of six argent and azure over all a bend gules (Annesley),
2nd, Argent a chevron between three escallops sable (Lyttleton), 3rd,
Gules a lion rampant within a bordure or (Talbot), 4th, qly i and iv
(France modern), ii and iii (England), all within a bordure compony
argent and azure (Beaufort)   In centre chief the Badge of Ulster
Earl's coronet   Crest: A Moor's head in profile couped at the
shoulders proper, wreathed at the temples argent and azure
Mantling: Azure and argent   Motto: Virtute amore
Supporters: Dexter, a Roman soldier in armour or, his exterior hand
resting on a shield bearing a female head proper   Sinister, a Moorish
soldier in armour or, in his exterior hand a bow proper
For George, 2nd Earl of Mountmorris, who m. 1790, Anne, dau. of
William, 2nd Viscount Courtenay, and d. 23 July 1844. (B.P. 1907 ed.)
(N.B. Only the husband's arms appear on the hatchment, which is
unusual)

2. All black background
On a lozenge   Annesley, impaling, Ermine three increscents gules (Sims)
Viscountess's coronet   Supporters: As 1.
For Frances Cockburn, dau. of Charles James Sims, who m. 1837,
George Arthur, Viscount Valentia, son and heir of George, 2nd Earl of
Mountmorris, and d. 21 Jan. 1856. (B.P. 1907 ed.)

ASTLEY

1. All black background
Sable a chevron three millpicks argent (Moseley), impaling, Gules a
lion rampant argent (? for Sockett)
Crest: An eagle displayed or ermined sable
Mantling: Gules and argent   Motto: In coelo quies
For Walter Michael Moseley, of the Mere, co. Worcs, who m. Anne
Elizabeth, dau. of Richard Sockett, of Worcester, and d. July, 1827.
She d. 1807.   (B.L.G. 1937 ed.)

BAYTON

1. Dexter background black
Qly, 1st and 4th, Paly of eight embattled argent and gules (Wigley), 2nd,
Azure on a fess between two lions passant or three cross crosslets fitchy
gules (Makepeace), 3rd, Per pale or and azure on a chevron three
martlets all counterchanged (Ludlam)   In pretence: Qly, 1st and 4th,
Argent a fess between three pierced cinquefoils sable (Meysey), 2nd and

3rd, Azure a fess vairy or and gules between three leopards' faces
jessant-de-lys or (Watkins)
Crest: Issuing from flames proper a tiger's head argent, maned sable,
gorged with a collar embattled gules
Mantling: Gules and argent   Motto: In coelo quies
For Edmund Meysey-Wigley, M.P. for Worcester, who m. 1795, Anna
Maria, dau. and heiress of Charles Watkins Meysey of Shakenhurst; he
assumed the additional name of Meysey in 1811, and d. 1821.
(Grazebrook 1873 ed.)

BEOLEY

1. All black background
On a lozenge (decorated quatrefoil)   Qly, 1st and 4th, Per pale argent
and vert three talbots courant counterchanged, on a chief gules an
eastern crown between two bugle horns stringed or (? Hunter), 2nd and
3rd, Argent a chevron engrailed azure in base a crescent gules
(? Alexander)
Unidentified

2. All black background
Argent a chevron engrailed azure ermined or, in base a crescent azure
(? Alexander)
Crest: On a nest proper a pelican in her piety or crowned with an
eastern coronet argent
Mantling: Azure and argent   Motto: Resurgam
Unidentified

3. Dexter background black
Qly, 1st and 4th, Per pale vert and gules three talbots courant argent,
on a chief argent an eastern crown between two bugle horns stringed
sable (? Hunter), 2nd and 3rd, Argent a chevron engrailed azure
ermined or, in base a crescent azure (? Alexander), impaling, Argent a
chevron between three bugle horns stringed sable (? Hornby)
Crests: Dexter, A falcon wings expanded and inverted proper, jessed,
belled and crowned with an eastern coronet or, standing on a bugle horn
sable and garnished or   Sinister, On a nest proper a pelican in her
piety or crowned with an ancient coronet argent
Mantling: Gules and argent   Motto: Resurgam
Unidentified

4. All black background
On a lozenge   Qly, 1st and 4th, (? Hunter) as 3., 2nd and 3rd,
(? Alexander) as 3., impaling, (? Hornby)
Unidentified

BESFORD

1. Dexter background black
Qly, 1st and 4th, Argent three cinquefoils sable (Sebright), 2nd, Per chevron sable and argent three elephants' heads erased counterchanged (Saunders), 3rd, Or a saltire gules over all a fess sable (Ashe); in fess point the Badge of Ulster: impaling, Argent three pallets gules within a bordure engrailed azure, on a canton argent a spur gules (Knight)
Crest: An heraldic tiger sejant argent, armed, maned and tufted or
Mantling: Gules and argent   Motto: Resurgam
For Sir John Sebright, 6th Bt. of Besford Court, who m. 1766, Sarah, dau. of Edward Knight of Wolverley, and d. Mar. 1794. (B.P. 1907 ed.) (There is a duplicate of this hatchment in the parish church at Flamstead, Herts.)

BEWDLEY

1. Sinister background black
Azure a fess argent between three pheons or (Malpas), impaling, Argent two bars gules over all a lion rampant sable (   )
Unidentified
This hatchment was removed from the demolished church of St. Andrew, Dowles, to the parish church in 1953.

BIRTSMORTON

1. All black background
Argent a chevron sable between three coots proper, in centre chief a molet sable (Coote)
Crest: A coot proper   Motto: Vincit veritas
Supporters: Two wolves sable ermined argent
For Richard, Lord Coloony, son of Richard, 3rd Earl of Bellamont. He d. unm. Oct. 1740.   (Burke's *Extinct Peerage*, 1866 ed.)

CROOME D'ABITOT

1. Dexter background black
Sable a fess ermine between three crescents or (Coventry), impaling, to dexter, Argent two lions passant gules (Lygon), and to sinister Qly, 1st and 4th, qly i and iv (France modern), ii & iii (England), 2nd, (Scotland), 3rd, (Ireland); over all a baton sinister gules charged with three roses argent barbed and seeded proper (Beauclerk)
Earl's coronet   On a mantle gules and ermine
Crest: A cock gules, combed, wattled and legged or, perched on a garb

fesswise or   Motto: Candida et constanter
Supporters: Two eagles with wings expanded argent, beaked and legged
or
For George William, 8th Earl of Coventry, who m. 1st, 1808, Emma
Susanna, 2nd dau. of William, 1st Earl Beauchamp; and 2nd, 1811,
Mary, dau.of Aubrey, 6th Duke of St Albans. He d. 15 May 1843.
(B.P. 1907 ed.)

CROOME ESTATE OFFICE

1. All black background
Coventry, impaling, to dexter, Gules on a fess between three doves
argent three crosses paty gules (Gunning), and to sinister, Argent on
a chief gules two molets or (St John)
Earl's coronet   Mantling: Gules and argent
Crest, motto and supporters: as for Coventry (see Croome d'Abitot)
For George William, 6th Earl of Coventry, who m. 1st, 1752, Maria,
dau. of John Gunning of co. Roscommon, and 2nd, 1764, Barbara,
dau. of John, 10th Baron St John of Bletsoe. He d. 3 Sept. 1809.
(B.P. 1907 ed.)

2. Dexter background black
Coventry   In pretence: Qly, 1st and 4th, Argent a barrulet between
two chevrons gules and three guttes sable (Pitches),. 2nd, Argent three
serpents embowed vert (Teague), 3rd, Argent three lions rampant gules
(Belhouse)
Crest, motto and supporters: As 1.
For George William, 7th Earl of Coventry, who m. 1st, 1777, Lady
Catherine Henley, dau. of Robert, Earl of Northington, and 2nd, 1783,
Peggy, dau. and co-heir of Sir Abraham Pitches.
He d. 1831. (B.P. 1907 ed.)

3. Dexter background black
Coventry, impaling, Or a leopard's face gules between two gamecocks
in pale proper between two flaunches sable (Cockerell)
Viscount's coronet   Mantling: Gules and argent
Crest and supporters: As 1.   Motto: Resurgam
For George William, Viscount Deerhurst, who m. 1836, Harriet Anne,
dau. of Sir Charles Cockerell, Bt., and d. 5 Nov. 1838.
 (B.P. 1907 ed.)

ELMLEY LOVETT

1. All black background
Qly, 1st and 4th, Qly per fess indented argent and sable in the first and
fourth quarters a bugle horn stringed sable garnished or (Forester), 2nd
and 3rd, Azure a chevron ermine between three escallops argent
(Townshend); in centre chief a crescent argent for cadency
Crest: A talbot passant argent collared sable, chained or
Mantling: Gules and argent   Motto: In coelo quies
For the Rev. Robert Townshend Forester of Elmley Lodge, who d. 27
July 1867. (Grazebrook 1873 ed.)

FLADBURY

1. Dexter background black
Gules three pears or, on a chief argent a demi-lion issuant sable
(Perrott), impaling, Argent three pallets embattled gules (Wigley)
Crest: A parrot vert, in the dexter claw a pear or leaved proper
Mantling: Gules and argent   Motto: Resurgam
For George Perrott of Craycombe House, who m. Jane, dau. of the
Rev. Henry Wigley of Pensham, and d. 5 Jan. 1806. (Grazebrook
1873 ed.)

2. Dexter background black
Perrott, impaling, Per fess sable and argent on a fess embattled-
counter-embattled between three gates three goats' heads erased
all counterchanged (Yates)
Crest: As 1.   Mantling: Vert and argent   Motto: In coelo quies
For George Wigley Perrott, who m. Charlotte Louisa Elisabeth, dau.
of Joseph Yates, and d. 1831.   She d. 1836.

3. All black background
Or a lion rampant within a bordure engrailed azure (Charlett)
Crest: A stag's head couped argent attired or, pierced through the neck
with an arrow argent   Mantling: Gules and argent
Unframed
For Arthur Charlett, J.P. who d. 25 April 1779, aged 86.
(Mural tablet)

GRAFTON FLYFORD

1. All black background
Azure on a fess engrailed between three swans' heads erased or ducally
gorged and langued gules three cinquefoils gules (Baker)
Crest: A dexter arm couped at the elbow proper holding a swan's head

erased or ducally gorged and langued gules
Mantling: Gules and argent   Motto: In coelo quies
Possibly for Thomas William Waldron Baker, son of John Baker of
Waresley, and May, only dau. of William Waldron of Hagley.
(Grazebrook 1873 ed.)

GRIMLEY

1. Dexter background black
Or a lion rampant gules (Griffiths), impaling, Gules a fess counter-
compony or and argent between thirteen billets seven in chief and six
in base argent (Lee)
Crest: A demi-lion rampant gules, langued, armed and crined azure
Mantling: Gules and argent   Motto: In coelo quies
For Richard Griffiths of Thorngrove Park, who m. Elizabeth Lee, of
Langley, co. Salop, and d. 1830. (Grazebrook 1873 ed. and mural
tablet)

2. All black background
On a lozenge
Griffiths impaling Lee, as 1.
For Elizabeth, widow of Richard Griffiths of Thorngrove Park.
She d. 1836. (Grazebrook 1873 ed.)

HALESOWEN

1. Dexter background black
Argent on a pale between two leopards' faces sable three crescents or
(Lea), impaling, Argent an eagle displayed gules armed or, on a chief
sable three bezants each bearing a fleur-de-lys azure (Grazebrook)
Crests: Dexter, An ostrich's head qly sable and argent between two
wings expanded gules, in the beak a horseshoe or (Smith)
Sinister, A unicorn passant argent gutty sable, gorged with a double
tressure flory-counter-flory gules (Lea)
Mantling: Gules and argent   Motto: In seipso totus teres
For Ferdinando Smith of Halesowen Grange (grandson of Anne, dau.
of William Lea of Halesowen), who m. 1st, Eliosa, dau. of Major
General St George Knudson, and 2nd, 1830, Elizabeth, dau. of
Michael Grazebrook of Audnam. He d. July 1841. (Grazebrook
1873 ed.)

HANLEY CASTLE, Severn End

1. Dexter background black
Qly, 1st and 4th, Gules a fess or in chief two pelicans or vulning them-
selves proper (Lechmere), 2nd, Vert fretty or (Whitmore), 3rd, Argent
three bears' heads erased sable muzzled or (Berwick); in fess point the
Badge of Ulster: impaling, Azure a martlet or between three molets
argent, all within a double tressure flory-counter-flory or (Murray)
Crest: A pelican azure vulning itself proper
Mantling: Gules and argent   Motto: Christus pelicano
Unframed
For Sir Edmund Hungerford Lechmere, 2nd Bt., who m. 1819, Maria
Clara, dau. of the Hon. David Murray, and d. 2 Apr. 1856.   (B.P.
1907 ed.)

2. Dexter background black
Lechmere, impaling, Argent on a fess double cotised gules three
griffins' heads erased or (Dashwood)
Crest: As 1.   Mantling: Gules and argent
Motto: Ducit amor patriae
For William Lechmere, of Steeple Aston, co. Oxford, who m. 1787,
Elizabeth, dau. of Sir John Dashwood-King, Bt. and d. 12 Dec. 1815.
(B.P. 1907 ed.)

HARTLEBURY

1. Sinister background black
Argent ten roundels gules (See of Worcester), impaling, Argent on a
chief or a raven proper (Hurd)
Shield surmounted by a mitre
Motto: Resurgam
For Richard Hurd, Bishop of Worcester, d. 1808. (Grazebrook 1873 ed.)

2. All black background
Azure on a fess engrailed between three swans' heads and necks erased
argent ducally gorged or three roses gules (Baker), impaling, Argent
three bulls' heads cabossed sable armed or (Waldron)
Crest: A dexter arm in armour embowed the hand proper holding a
swan's head and neck erased argent ducally gorged or
Mantling: Gules and argent   Motto: Resurgam
For John Baker, of Waresley, who m. Mary, dau. of William Waldron of
Hagley, and d.   (Grazebrook 1873 ed.)

KIDDERMINSTER

1. All black background
Lozengy or and azure a chevron gules charged with a crescent or for
cadency (Gorges)
Crest: A greyhound's head erased sable collared or
Mantling: Gules and or   Motto: Memento mori
For Henry Gorges, second son of John Gorges of Somerset.
He d. 24 May 1658.   (Parish registers)

KYRE WYARD

1. Sinister background black
Qly, 1st, Gules a chevron ermine between three eagles close argent
(Childe), 2nd, Qly per fess indented ermine and azure (Lacon), 3rd,
Argent a saltire sable (Baldwin), 4th, Azure three bars argent in chief
three estoiles or (Pytts), impaling, Qly, 1st and 4th, Ermine a fret
sable (Cludde), 2nd and 3rd, Argent a bend double cotised sable in
chief a martlet sable (Orleton)
For Harriet, younger dau. of William Cludde of Orleton, who m. 1807,
William Lacon Childe of Kyre Park and Kinlet.   She d. 1849.
(B.L.G. 1937 ed.)

2. Dexter background black
Pytts, impaling, Gules an inescutcheon argent within an orle of molets
or (Chamberlayne)
Crest: A dove with wings displayed argent within a circular wreath of
wheat or; above the crest the motto 'Pax et plenitudino'
Mantling: Gules and argent   Motto: In coelo quies
For Jonathan Pytts, who m. Annabella, dau. of Edmund Chamberlayne
of Maugersbury, co. Gloucester, and d.s.p. Nov. 1807. (Nash,
History of Worcestershire, 1781)

LITTLE MALVERN PRIORY

1. Dexter background black
Sable three greyhounds courant in pale argent collared gules within a
bordure gules (Berington), impaling, Qly, 1st and 4th, Purpure three
bars argent (Brun), 2nd and 3rd, Azure three bells or (   )
Crest: A greyhound's head couped argent collared gules
Mantling: Gules and argent   Motto: Resurgam
For William Berington, who m. 1824, Mary Frances, only child of
Don Josef Brun of Cadiz, and d. 16 Apr. 1847. (B.L.G. 1937 ed.)

2. Sinister background black

Berington, in chief a crescent argent, impaling, Gules on a bend argent three molets sable (?Balfe)

Motto: Mihi autem ausit gloriare nisi in cruce DNIC

(The shield is held by an angel, standing behind the shield)

Probably for Ellen Mary, dau. of James Balfe of Runnymede, co. Roscommon, who m. 1858, Charles Michael Berington, and d.s.p. 18 Aug. 1866.   (B.L.G. 1937 ed.)

3. All black background

On a lozenge   Qly, 1st and 4th, Argent a cross moline engrailed sable between four Cornish choughs proper, on a chief azure a boar's head couped proper (Williams), 2nd and 3rd, Argent a chevron between three cross crosslets fitchy sable within a bordure gules bezanty (Russell) Unidentified

4. All black background

On a lozenge   Vert a saltire wavy ermine (Wakeman)   In pretence: Qly, 1st and 4th, Gules a cross double-parted flory ancient between four martlets or, on a chief argent a boar's head couped sable (Williams), 2nd, Russell, 3rd, Or on a bend sable three molets or (Monington)

For Mary, dau. and heiress of Thomas Williams of Trellynic, co. Flint, who m. 1796, Walter Wakeman, son of Henry Wakeman of Beckford, co. Gloucester, and d. 1828.   (B.L.G. 1937 ed.)

5. Dexter background black

Wakeman, with escutcheon of pretence as 4., but cross moline in Williams coat

Crest: A lion's head erased or vomiting flames proper

Motto: In coelo quies

For Walter Wakeman, husband of Mary Williams. He d.s.p. 1800. (B.L.G. 1937 ed.)

NORTON-WITH-LENCHWICK

1. Dexter background black

Qly, 1st and 4th, Argent a fess between six cross crosslets fitchy gules (Craven), 2nd and 3rd, Or five fleurs-de-lys in cross sable a chief wavy azure (Craven ancient); at fess point a crescent sable for cadency: impaling, Qly, 1st, Argent three bars gemel gules, over all a lion rampant sable (Fairfax), 2nd, Argent a chevron between three foxes' heads erased gules (Fairfax), 3rd, Barry of eight argent and gules, on a canton sable a cross patonce or (Etton), 4th, Argent on a fess sable between three fleurs-de-lys gules three bezants (Thwaites)

Crest: On a chapeau gules and ermine a griffin statant, wings elevated

ermine, beaked and membered or
Mantling: Gules and argent   Motto: Mors iter ad vitam
For Sir William Craven of Lenchwick, who m. Elizabeth, dau. of
Ferdinando, 2nd Baron Fairfax of Cameron, and d. 12 Oct. 1655.
(B.P. 1907 ed.)

OMBERSLEY, Private Chapel of Lord Sandys

1. Dexter background black

Qly, 1st, Or a fess dancetty between three cross crosslets fitchy gules
(Sandys), 2nd, Or on a bend engrailed vert three pheons or (Tipping),
3rd, Argent three crescents gules (Cheek), 4th, Argent a lion rampant
gules, on a chief sable three escallops argent (Russell), impaling, Gules
a lion rampant ermine ducally crowned or, on a chief or three
martlets sable (Colebrooke)
Baron's coronet   Motto: Probum non poenitet
Supporters: Two griffins per fess or and gules collared dancetty gules
For Edwin, 2nd Baron Sandys, D.C.L., M.P., who m. 1769, Anna Maria,
dau. of James Colebrooke of Southgate, Middlesex, and d.s.p. 11 Mar.
1797.   (B.P. 1907 ed.)

2. All black background

On a lozenge   Qly, 1st, Sandys, 2nd, Tipping, 3rd, Cheek, 4th,
Russell, impaling, Colebrooke
Baroness's coronet   Supporters: As 1.
For Anna Maria, widow of Edwin, 2nd Baron Sandys.   She d. 1 Nov.
1806.   (B.P. 1907 ed.)

3. All black background

Two lozenges   Dexter lozenge: Qly, 1st, Sable on a fess argent
between three leopards passant guardant or spotted sable three
escallops gules (Hill), 2nd, Per bend sinister ermine and sable ermined
argent a lion rampant or (Trevor), 3rd, Gules a cinquefoil or (Rowe),
4th, Argent a chevron azure between three trefoils slipped gules
(Rowe)   In pretence: Sandys
Marchioness's coronet   Supporters: Dexter, A leopard or, spotted
sable, ducally gorged and chained gules   Sinister, A reindeer gules,
attired, unguled and collared or
Sinister lozenge: Qly, 1st, Sandys, 2nd, Tipping, 3rd, Cheek, 4th,
Russell
Baroness's coronet   Supporters: As 1.   All on a mantle gules and
ermine
For Mary, dau. of the Hon. Martyn Sandys, who m. 1786, Arthur, 2nd
Marquess of Downshire. She was created Baroness Sandys of
Ombersley, 1802, and d. 1 Aug. 1836.   (B.P. 1907 ed.)

4. All black background

Sandys
Baron's coronet   Crest: A griffin segreant per fess or and gules
Motto: Probum non poenitet
Supporters: As 1.
For Lieut. General Arthur Moyses William, 2nd Baron Sandys, who d.
unm. 16 July 1860.   (B.P. 1907 ed.)

5. Dexter background black

Sandys, impaling, Argent a chevron sable between three garbs or (Blake)
Baron's coronet   Crest, motto and supporters: As 4.
For Arthur Marcus Cecil, 3rd Baron Sandys, P.C., who m. 1837, Louisa,
youngest dau. of Joseph Blake, and d. 10 Apr. 1863.   (B.P. 1907 ed.)

PERSHORE Abbey

1. All black background

Ermine on a fess gules a lion passant or (Probyn), impaling, two coats
per fess: in chief, Qly, 1st and 4th, Gules three eagles' legs erased or
(Bund), 2nd and 3rd, Azure a chevron ermine between three cross
crosslets fitchy argent (Parsons); in base, Or on a chevron between three
molets of six points gules a cross paty or (Willis)
Crest: An ostrich's head erased proper, ducally gorged, and holding in
the beak a key or
Mantling: Gules and argent   Motto: In coelo quies
For the Rev. William Probyn, Vicar of Pershore, who m. 1st, 1787,
Mary, dau. of William Bund of Wick; she d. 1802. He m. 2nd, Sarah,
dau. of John Willis, and d. 1 Apr. 1825.   (Mural tablet)

2. All black background

Argent three bears' paws couped erect within a bordure engrailed sable
(Bedford), impaling, Azure a chevron chequy or and gules between
three cinquefoils argent, on a chief ermine a catherine wheel gules
(Jenner)
Crest: A demi-lion rampant sable murally crowned or, holding between
the paws a bezant
Mantling: Gules and or   Motto: Resurgam
For John Yeend Bedford, of the Abbey, Pershore, who m. 1822,
Catherine, only dau. of Edward Jenner, M.D., and d. 11 May, 1854.
(Grazebrook 1873 ed. and mural tablet)

3. Dexter background black

Azure three boars' heads couped within an orle of cross crosslets argent
(Cradock)   In pretence: Chequy or and gules (?Fitzwarren)
Crest: On a dexter gauntlet sable a boar's head couped argent, pierced

by a sword paleways proper hilted or
Mantling: Gules and argent   Motto: Mors est omnibus communis
Probably for William Cradock, as it hangs over the mural tablet
recording his death in 1782 at the age of 42.

QUEENHILL

1. All black background

Ermine two bars sable charged with three bezants, 2 and 1, on a canton
argent a chief sable charged with a cross paty between two martlets or
(Tennant)
Crest: A lion passant guardant proper the dexter paw resting on an
escutcheon ermine, thereon two bars charged as in the arms
Mantling: None (shield surrounded by decorative scrollwork)
For William Tennant, who d. unm. 1848 at Ham Court, and was buried
at Queenhill.   (B.L.G. 1937 ed.)

SHRAWLEY

1. Dexter background black

Or on a fess azure three garbs or in chief a cross crosslet fitchy gules
(Vernon), impaling, Azure two bars wavy argent in chief a lion passant
guardant or (Tayler)
Crest: A demi-woman proper, habited purpure, crined or, in the arms a
garb or   Motto: Resurgam
For Thomas Shrawley Vernon of Hanbury Hall, who m. 1790,
Elizabeth, dau. of the Rev. John Tayler, and d. 17 Mar. 1825.
(B.P. 1907 ed.)

2. Dexter background black

Argent on a chevron between three griffins' heads erased sable langued
gules three molets or (?Cliffe), impaling, Gules a lion rampant or within
a bordure vair (?Skrymshaw)
Crest: A griffin passant argent, wings addorsed, beaked and forelegs
or, langued gules   Mantling: Gules and ermine   Motto: Vive et vivas
Unidentified

SOUTH LITTLETON

1. All black background

Sable a lion statant argent (Taylor), impaling, Sable three swords
fessways in pale argent hilted or (Rawlins)
Crest: An ounce statant proper   Mantling: Gules and ermine
For Rev. Francis Taylor, D.D., who m. Elizabeth, dau. of William

Rawlins, of Salford, co. Warwick, and d. Mar. 1722. (Grazebrook 1873 ed.)

SPETCHLEY

1. All black background
Gules a chevron between ten crosses paty, six and four, argent (Berkeley), impaling, Azure on a fess cotised or three leopards' faces gules (Lee)
Crest: A bear's head argent muzzled gules
Mantling: Gules and argent   Motto: Resurgam
For Robert Berkeley, who m. 1792, Apollonia, 3rd dau. of Richard Lee, of Llanfoist, co. Monmouth, and d. 14 Dec. 1804.   (B.L.G. 1937 ed. and mural tablet)

2. All black background
Berkeley, impaling, Azure a chevron between three pears or (Benfield)
Crest: As 1.
Mantling: Gules and argent   Motto: Requiescat in pace
For Robert Berkeley, J.P., D.L., who m. 1822, Henrietta Sophia, dau. of Paul Benfield, and d. 1874.   (B.L.G. 1937 ed.)

3. Sinister background black
Berkeley impaling Benfield
Mantling: Gules and argent   Motto: Dieu avec nous
For Henrietta Sophia, wife of Robert Berkeley. She d. 1857. (B.L.G. 1937 ed.)

STOULTON

1. Dexter background black
Gules a fess within a bordure engrailed ermine (Acton)
Crest: An arm embowed in armour proper holding in the hand a sword argent, thereon a boar's head couped sable, distilling blood proper
Mantling: Gules and argent   Motto: In coelo quies
Probably for William Acton, of Little Wolverton, who m. 1801, Ann Constantia Davies of St. Thomas, co. Stafford, and d. 1814. (B.L.G. 1937 ed. and mural tablet)

STOURBRIDGE, Oldswinford Hospital

1. All black background
Argent a fess engrailed between three cinquefoils sable, all within a bordure sable (Foley)

Crest: A lion rampant argent holding between the forepaws an escutcheon of the arms
Mantling: Gules and argent   Motto: Vince malum bono
Probably the hatchment of William Foley, great-great-grandson of Thomas Foley, founder of the Hospital. He d. unm. 1756.
(Burke's *Extinct Baronetcies* 1844 ed.)

STRENSHAM

1. All black background
Ermine on a chief indented sable three escallops or (Taylor)
Crest: A demi-lion ermine holding between the paws an escallop or
Motto: Fidelisque ad mortem
For John Taylor of Strensham, High Sheriff of Worcestershire, 1817.
He d.s.p. 3 Aug. 1848.   (Mural tablet)

2. Dexter background black
Ermine on a chief dancetty sable three escallops or (Taylor)
In pretence: Azure a fess ermine between three estoiles of eight points or (Skey)   Also impaling, Qly, 1st and 4th, Sable a chevron between three millpicks argent (Moseley), 2nd, Qly per fess dancetty sable and argent in the first quarter a lion passant guardant or (Croft), 3rd, Gules semy of cross crosslets fitchy or two lions passant in pale argent (Acton)
Crest: As 1.   Mantling: Gules and argent   Motto: As 1.
For James Taylor of Moseley Hall, who m. 1st, 1814, Louisa, dau. and heiress of Samuel Skey of Bewdley, and 2nd, 1825, Ann Elizabeth, eldest dau. of Walter Michael Moseley of Buildwas Park, co. Salop.
He was High Sheriff of Worcestershire in 1826, and d. 8 Oct. 1852.
(B.L.G. 1937 ed.)
(There is a duplicate of this hatchment in the parish church of Kings Norton, Warwickshire)

WOLVERLEY

1. Dexter background black
Azure on a fess argent, between three martlets in chief and the Roman fasces erect surmounting two swords in saltire and encircled by a chaplet in base or, three chess rooks sable (Brown)   In pretence: Argent a chevron sable between three gamecocks proper armed gules (   )
Crest: A demi-eagle displayed with two heads azure, charged on the breast with the fasces, swords and chaplet as in the arms
Mantling: Gules and argent   Motto: Fortiter et fideliter
For John Brown of Lea Castle, who was High Sheriff in 1833, and

d. 1845.   (Grazebrook 1873 ed.)

2. All black background
On a lozenge   Brown, with escutcheon of pretence as 1.
Motto: Resurgam
For the widow of John Brown.   She d. 1846.   (Grazebrook 1873
ed.)

3. Dexter background black
Qly, 1st and 4th, Argent two barrulets dancetty sable between three
Saracens' heads couped at the shoulder proper (Westhead), 2nd and 3rd,
Brown   In pretence: Per chevron or and azure, in chief a molet of six
points between two crosses paty azure, and in base the front elevation
of a chapel argent (Chappell)
Crests: Dexter, Within a fetterlock or a Saracen's head couped proper
wreathed round the temples argent and sable   Sinister, as 1.
Mantling: Sable and argent   Motto: Ora et labora
For Joshua Proctor Brown-Westhead, who m. Betsy, dau. of George
Royle Chappell, of Nelson House, Manchester, and d. 1877.
(Grazebrook 1873 ed.)

4. Dexter background black
Qly, 1st, qly i and iv (Westhead), ii and iii (Brown), 2nd, Brown, 3rd,
Westhead, 4th, Chappell, impaling, Or a lion rampant between three
swans' heads erased, all within a bordure invected azure charged with
eight annulets or (Thompson)
Crests: Dexter, Westhead   Sinister, Brown
Mantling: Sable and or   Motto: Ora et labora
For Marcus Brown-Westhead, who m. 1835, Frances Mary, dau. of
John Cator Thompson, of Bazil Grange, West Derby, and d. 1897.
(Grazebrook 1873 ed.)

5. All black background
On a lozenge   Argent three eagles displayed gules ducally crowned
or (Kingsale), impaling, Qly, 1st and 4th, qly i and iv (Westhead), ii
and iii (Brown), 2nd and 3rd, Chappell
Baron's coronet   Supporters: Two unicorns azure each gorged with
coronets composed of crosses paty and fleurs-de-lys, chained, armed,
crined and unguled or
For Adelaide, only dau. of Joshua Proctor Brown-Westhead of Lea
Castle, who m. Mar. 1855, John Constantine, 29th Baron Kingsale,
and d. 21 Jan. 1885.   (B.P. 1907 ed.)

Worcestershire hatchments in the county, privately owned but no longer in the parishes to which they originally belonged.

1. Dexter background black
Argent an orle between eight martlets sable (Winnington), in centre chief the Badge of Ulster, impaling, Ermine on a chief indented sable three escallops or (Taylor)
Crest: A Saracen's head proper couped at the shoulders and wreathed about the shoulders argent and sable
Mantling: Gules and argent   Motto: In coelo quies
For Sir Thomas Edward Winnington, 3rd Bt. of Stanford Court, Stourport, Worcs, who m. 1810, Joanna, eldest dau. of John Taylor, J.P., D.L. of Moseley Hall, and d. 24 Sept. 1839.
(B.P. 1907 ed.)
(In the possession of Mr W.A. Peplow, Wych Garth, Dingle Road, Pedmore, Stourbridge)

2. All black background
Qly, 1st and 4th, Or fretty gules a canton ermine (Noel), 2nd and 3rd, Or fretty gules three pears or, on a chief argent a demi-lion issuant sable (Perrott), impaling, Argent on a chief azure three martlets or (Wylde)
Crest: (on a peer's helm) A buck at gaze argent attired or
Mantling: Gules and argent   Motto: Jus suum cuique
For Charles Noel, J.P., D.L. of Bell Hall, Belbroughton, co. Worcs., who m. 1828, Mary, dau. of the Rev. John Wylde, Rector of Aldridge, co. Stafford, and d. 3 Feb. 1877. (Grazebrook 1873 ed.)
(In the possession of Mr W.A. Peplow)

Non-Worcestershire hatchments in the county

1. All black background
Two lozenges   Dexter, Argent a saltire gules a chief ermine
(Fitzmaurice)   In pretence: Qly, 1st, Azure a ship at anchor oars in
saltire within a double tressure flory-counter-flory or (Orkney), 2nd and
3rd, qly i & iv, Gules three cinquefoils ermine (Hamilton), ii & iii,
Argent a ship sails furled sable (Arran), 4th, Argent a human heart
imperially crowned proper, on a chief azure three molets argent
(Douglas)   The escutcheon of pretence surmounted by a countess's
coronet   Sinister, A lozenge with the arms as on escutcheon of
pretence   Both lozenges on a mantle gules and ermine surmounted
by a countess's coronet
Supporters: Dexter, An antelope argent, armed, ducally gorged, chained and
unguled or Sinister, A stag proper, attired, unguled, collared and chained or
For Mary O'Bryen, 3rd Countess of Orkney, who m. 1777, the Hon.
Thomas Fitzmaurice, 2nd son of John, Earl of Shelburne, and d. 30 Dec.
1831.   He d. 1793. (B.P. 1907 ed.)
(In the possession of Mrs. R.H. Butler, Brockencote Hall, Chaddesley
Corbett)

2. Dexter background black
Qly, 1st and 4th, Or a fret azure (Eyton), 2nd and 3rd, Gules two bars
ermine (Pantulf), impaling, Gyronny of eight or and sable (Campbell)
Crests: Centre, A reindeer's head couped attired or in its mouth an
acorn slipped vert fructed or   Dexter, A Cornish chough's head
erased proper in the beak a trefoil slipped vert
Sinister, A lion's head argent devouring a barrel or
Mantling: Gules and argent   Motto: Je m'y oblige
For Thomas Eyton of Eyton, Salop, who m. 1808, Elizabeth, eldest
dau. of Major General Donald Campbell, and d. 13 Feb. 1855.
(B.L.G. 1937 ed.)
(In the possession of Mr W.A. Peplow, Wych Garth, Dingle Road,
Pedmore, Stourbridge)

3. Dexter background black
Ermine on a fess sable three molets argent (Lyster), impaling, Qly, 1st
and 4th, Argent three bulls passant sable armed and unguled or
(Ashley), 2nd and 3rd, Gules a bend engrailed between six lions
rampant or (Cooper)
Crest: A stag's head couped proper
Mantling: Gules and argent   Motto: Loyal au mort
For Henry Lyster of Rowton Castle, Salop, who m. 1824, Charlotte
Barbara, 3rd dau. of the 6th Earl of Shaftesbury, and d. 12 Dec. 1863.
(B.P. 1907 ed.)
(In the possession of Mr W.A. Peplow)

4. All black background

Qly, 1st and 4th, Per fess argent and sable a pale between three griffins' heads erased all counterchanged (Gardner), 2nd Per pale azure and purpure a cross engrailed or between four roses argent barbed vert (Burton), 3rd, Sable on a bend between six cross crosslets fitchy argent three bugle horns stringed sable (Horner), impaling. Argent a chevron between three buckets sable, hoops and handles or (Pemberton)
Crest: A griffin's head erased sable langued gules
Mantling: Gules and argent   Motto: In coelo quies
Probably for the Rev. Laurence Gardner, D.D. of Sansaw, Shrewsbury, Salop, who m. 1799, Martha Pemberton, and d. 26 July 1843.
(Morris' Genealogy of Shropshire)
(In the possession of Mr W.A. Peplow)

5. All black background

Or a lion rampant sable a label of five point gules (Dampier)
Crest: A demi-lion sable ducally crowned or
Mantling: Gules and argent
On motto scroll: "The Arms of Dampier"
Perhaps for Captain William Dampier who d.s.p. 1715.
(Tentative identification based on no authority other than family tradition)
(In the possession of Mrs Bennett, Worcester)

SELECT BIBLIOGRAPHY

W.A. Peplow, 'Hatchments in Worcestershire,' in *Worcs. Arch. Soc.*, vol. 32, (1956), 1–12, and XXXIII (1957), 1–13.

P.G. Summers, *How to read a Coat of Arms*, (National Council of Social Service, 1967), 17–20.

P.G. Summers, *The Genealogists' Magazine*, vol. 12, No. 13 (1958), 443–446.

T.D.S. Bayley and F.W. Steer, 'Painted Heraldic Panels', in *Antiquaries Journal*, vol. 35 (1955), 68–87.

L.B. Ellis, 'Royal Hatchments in City Churches', in *London and Middlesex Arch. Soc. Transactions* (New Series, vol. 10 1948), 24–40 (contains extracts from a herald-painter's work-book relating to hatchments and eighteenth century funerals).

C.A. Markham, 'Hatchments', in *Northampton & Oakham Architectural Soc. Proceedings*, vol. 20, Pt. 2 (1912), 673–687.

INDEX OF NAMES